TRADING ON CORPORATE EARNINGS NEWS

TRADING ON CORPORATE EARNINGS NEWS

PROFITING FROM TARGETED, SHORT-TERM OPTIONS POSITIONS

JOHN SHON
PING ZHOU

Vice President, Publisher: Tim Moore
Associate Publisher and Director of Marketing: Amy Neidlinger
Executive Editor: Jim Boyd
Editorial Assistant: Pamela Boland
Operations Manager: Gina Kanouse
Senior Marketing Manager: Julie Phifer
Publicity Manager: Laura Czaja
Assistant Marketing Manager: Megan Colvin
Cover Designer: Chuti Prasertsith
Managing Editor: Kristy Hart
Project Editor: Anne Goebel
Copy Editor: Gayle Johnson
Proofreader: Debbie Williams
Senior Indexer: Cheryl Lenser
Compositor: TnT Design, Inc.
Manufacturing Buyer: Dan Uhrig

FT Press offers excellent discounts on this book when ordered in quantity for bulk purchases or special sales. For more information, please contact U.S. Corporate and Government Sales, 1-800-382-3419, corpsales@pearsontechgroup.com. For sales outside the U.S., please contact International Sales at international@pearson.com.

First Printing March 2011

ISBN-10: 0-13-708492-7
ISBN-13: 978-0-13-708492-0

Pearson Education LTD.
Pearson Education Australia PTY, Limited
Pearson Education Singapore, Pte. Ltd.
Pearson Education Asia, Ltd.
Pearson Education Canada, Ltd.
Pearson Educatión de Mexico, S.A. de C.V.
Pearson Education—Japan
Pearson Education Malaysia, Pte. Ltd.

Library of Congress Cataloging-in-Publication Data

Shon, John, 1971-
   Trading on corporate earnings news : profiting from targeted, short-term options positions / John Shon, Ping Zhou.
      p. cm.
   Includes bibliographical references and index.
   ISBN 978-0-13-708492-0 (hbk. : alk. paper)
   1. Speculation. 2. Corporate profits. 3. Price-earnings ratio. 4. Investment analysis. I. Zhou, Ping, 1973- II. Title.
   HG6041.S486 2011
   332.63'2283—dc22
                                                     2010044969

To Mom and Dad and Lucy   —John

*To Rong, for having faith in me and supporting
me unconditionally; and to Kelly, for filling
my world with joy   —Ping*

Contents

PART III: EVIDENCE: MARKET REACTIONS

PART IV: IMPLEMENTATION: OPTIONS TRADING STRATEGIES

Acknowledgments

We thank our editor, Jim Boyd, for his invaluable guidance, experience, and encouragement. We also want to extend our appreciation to two reviewers, Jeff Augen and Michael Thomsett. Jeff and Michael helped improve the book's readability and provided valuable insights into how to provide the most value to our readers. We also thank the project editor, Anne Goebel, and the entire production crew at Pearson.

We also thank many of our friends and colleagues in academia and the investment management industry. Although we did not directly interact with them on this project, their intellectual influence on us over the years is certainly reflected in our work. Our book has also benefited greatly from the decades of academic research in accounting, finance, and economics; the list of the individual authors of these studies is certainly too long to be displayed here.

Finally, we want to especially thank our families for their support.

From John: I want to thank my parents for constantly pushing, and Lucy for constantly pulling.

From Ping: I want to thank my wife, Rong, for having faith in me and giving me unconditional love and support, without which I would not have been able to finish this project. This book is also for my daughter, Kelly. She is only six months old and may have limited interest in options trading at this stage of her life, but she inspires me and fills my world with joy.

About the Authors

John Shon is a professor of accounting at Fordham University. He has a PhD in accounting and an MBA in finance from the University of Chicago Booth School of Business. He publishes extensively in academic journals and has received several grants and awards for his research on equity markets. He teaches at the Gabelli School of Business and the Graduate School of Business Administration. He has received several teaching awards throughout his career.

Ping Zhou is a portfolio manager and vice president of the Quantitative Investment Group at Neuberger Berman (formerly Lehman Brothers Asset Management). He manages U.S. and global equity funds for institutional investors. He has a PhD in accounting from Georgia State University. His expertise is in portfolio theory, market anomalies, investor behavior, corporate finance, and risk management. Before joining the industry, he was an accounting professor at City University of New York–Baruch College. He has published numerous studies about the equity markets and corporate finance in academic journals, including *Financial Analysts Journal, Journal of Investing, Journal of Accounting, Auditing and Finance, Journal of Accounting and Public Policy*, and *Review of Quantitative Finance and Accounting*. He has received several awards for his research, including the Distinguished Paper Award at the 2007 annual meeting of the Mid-Atlantic region of American Accounting Association.

Preface

KISS

All books are largely an extension of their authors. So we'd like to briefly describe ourselves and thus inform you, the reader, about our perspective.

Ping Zhou is a portfolio manager for the Quantitative Investment Group at Neuberger Berman, a major asset management firm. He is a true "quant" who uses sophisticated statistical, empirical models to squeeze profits out of the market. His days are spent with fellow PhDs, performing the highest levels of quantitative analysis. He has access to an incredible arsenal of computing power and resources.

John Shon is a professor of accounting at Fordham University. He was formally trained for his doctorate at the University of Chicago's Booth School of Business in high-level theoretical and quantitative analysis, under Nobel laureates in economics and finance. He spends his days performing cutting-edge academic research using sophisticated statistical procedures, and he regularly publishes in top academic journals.

On the surface, the two of us are in very different fields. Yet, one of our commonalities is our exposure to quantitative sophistication. Perhaps ironically, then, one of the key traits we share is our belief that, in certain scenarios, rigorous quantitative analysis can be overdone. We believe in Leonardo da Vinci's famous saying:

"Simplicity is the ultimate sophistication." Put differently, we believe in the adage commonly referred to as KISS: "Keep it simple, stupid." This shared philosophy is at the core of our writings. Many options-trading books overwhelm the reader with what we believe are unnecessary complexities. In this book, we whittle to the bare essentials the types of trades that will be profitable. We have made every effort to pare away complexities and show the essence of each trade. As such, we spend very little time discussing the greeks of options analysis—delta, gamma, theta, rho. Don't get us wrong: understanding the greeks is important for a full understanding of your trades. However, we believe that many of these issues can obfuscate and distract you from our main task at hand, so we suggest that you acquire this information elsewhere to supplement the material we cover here. Two excellent books that cover basic concepts are *Options Made Easy* and *The Bible of Options Strategies*, both by Guy Cohen. They'll provide you with some of the foundational knowledge you'll need. Two essential books that cover advanced concepts are *The Volatility Edge in Options Trading* and *Day Trading Options*, both by Jeff Augen. They discuss many of the volatility-related issues that you'll want to deal with, as well as the details of intraday trading.

The Importance of Theory

The other key trait that we as coauthors share is our firm belief in developing strong, foundational economic understanding of and intuition about the world around us. This arises partially from our doctoral training. But it also arises from our common interest in simply *under-standing* how and why markets function the way they do. We therefore put strong emphasis on understanding the theory behind our trades and why we believe in them. We also put heavy emphasis on findings that are statistically tested and empirically documented, not on conjectures that are backed by cherry-picked trades or hearsay from random investing/trading blogs.

How does this affect the writing in this book? Simply put, if we did not share this philosophy of stressing the economic theory and empirical findings behind our trading strategies, we would not have had to write the underlying theories presented in Chapters 2 through 6 (and, to a lesser extent, Chapters 12 through 15). If you are simply interested in knowing the basic trading strategies that this book recommends, you need look no further than Chapters 9, 10, and 11. However, if you're interested in developing a deeper understanding of the markets and one of the most salient, important, recurring events that occurs in equity markets—earnings announcements—this book provides a wealth of information. *Economic theory. Empirical evidence.* This is the intellectual heavy lifting that we encourage you to do with us.

Not Just for Options Trading

Because of the depth of economic theory and empirical evidence that we cover in this book, you will find that the material is not limited to options trading. Rather, the deeper understanding you gain about the nature of earnings announcements and earnings surprises will also equip you to understand the underlying *stock* price reactions. Therefore, the material is also suited for readers who do not regularly trade options. This book contains many ideas that stock-based investors will find immensely helpful in their approach to trading.

Preview of Chapters

Chapters 2 through 4 discuss the latest cutting-edge academic research on earnings announcements and earnings surprises. This is theory and empirical evidence garnered from decades of research using millions of publicly traded observations on earnings releases. Chapters 5 and 6 discuss the theory and evidence behind market reactions to earnings announcements, as well as the earnings surprises that these announcements create. The empirical regularities of market reactions to earnings announcements and earnings surprises represent the foundation from which we develop our options-based trades. Chapter 7 discusses some of the empirical evidence on optioned firms and then discusses the specific behavior of options around earnings announcements. Chapter 8 talks about some of the practical issues related to implementing your trades. Chapters 9 through 11 discuss our main options-based trading strategies. These strategies are short-term trades that are targeted at companies' quarterly earnings announcements. These three chapters represent the bulk of the discussion on options trades, using actual examples from recent earnings announcements. Chapters 12 through 15 discuss several other theories and empirical regularities that will help you improve the odds of implementing profitable options trades.

After reading this book, you will be better informed about the theoretical underpinnings of earnings announcements. We believe this foundational work is paramount to being a consistently profitable trader. As trading situations and economic contexts change, your foundational understanding will always be there to help you adapt. As the old saying goes, we don't want to just give you a fish; we want to show you how to fish.

Part I

Introduction

Chapter 1

Introduction

A recent study by Roll, Schwartz, and Subrahmanyam (2009) found that *options trading around earnings announcements* has been steadily increasing every year from 1996 to 2007. So, you're in good company. This is one of the main reasons we decided to write this book. The other reason is the trading experience of a dear friend of ours—let's call him Bob.

The Stock-Based Trade

Let us tell you about our friend, Bob, who lost a lot of money on a trading position. Near market close on September 24, 2009, Bob decided to buy shares of Research in Motion (NASDAQ: RIMM). Following Warren Buffett's philosophy, he liked the story behind Research in Motion, a Canadian high-tech company that practically cornered the market in push technology handheld devices: the ubiquitous BlackBerry. Bob liked that all his friends who were once BlackBerry-less now strutted around with the device. He liked that the company's P/E

3

ratio was much lower than Apple's. In short, Bob was convinced that Research in Motion would have a great future. What was especially interesting about Bob's RIMM trade was the timing of his purchase—only a few hours before RIMM was scheduled to make its earnings announcement for the second quarter of 2009.

Bob bought 200 shares of RIMM at the market close price of $83.06. After close on that day, RIMM made its earnings announcement. Earnings per share (EPS) was $1.03, beating the consensus EPS forecast of $1.00. Revenues for the quarter were $3.42 billion, a 37% increase from a year earlier, but below what analysts were expecting. Moreover, the company issued earnings and revenue guidance for the rest of the year that was lower than expected. Collectively, the earnings announcement had a mix of good news and bad news: Earnings were better than expected, but revenues were worse than expected—yet revenue growth was still very strong. The next day, RIMM opened at $70.48, a decline of $12.58 per share, or −15.2% (see Figure 1.1). Bob's 200 shares of RIMM, representing an initial investment of $16,612, lost $2,516. Ouch.

Bob did what many of us have done in the past with our equity trades. He tried to time the market. In particular, he tried to time the market around an earnings announcement. We don't think this is a bad idea per se. Indeed, we'll make the point that it can be quite a good idea, but only under the right circumstances and with the right tools. A disproportionately large portion of the returns that a stock makes during a given year is centered around its four quarterly earnings announcements.[1] Our own analysis (which we discuss in detail later) shows that half of the earnings announcements made by companies have market returns that are *30 times as large* as a typical no-announcement day. These large earnings-announcement returns naturally lend themselves to trading. And although trading in the company's stock is one way to do it, in this book, we design *option*-based strategies that can be extremely profitable—regardless of the direction of the market's reaction.

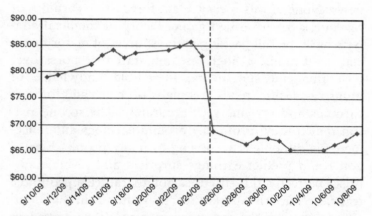

FIGURE 1.1 *Research in Motion (NASDAQ: RIMM) stock price in the 20 trading days surrounding the earnings announcement*

Another aspect of Bob's trade was that he was on the wrong side of the trade: His prediction of the direction of the market reaction to RIMM's earnings announcement was simply wrong. Although he correctly predicted that RIMM's reported earnings would be better than expectations, he didn't accurately predict the fall in RIMM's revenue or its lowered guidance for the next quarter. In hindsight, this is not all that surprising. As Nils Bohr, a Nobel laureate in physics, famously said, "Prediction is very difficult, especially if it is about the future."

Earnings Surprises and Opposite-Direction Market Reactions

If we really think about what Bob was trying to do here, we would realize that he was facing a daunting task. For his trade to be profitable, he had to be correct about the earnings and revenue surprises, the change in guidance, and, most importantly, the market's reaction to all this news. None of this is easy. First, forecasting earnings or revenue is a very tough game. Plenty of financial analysts have the full backing and resources of major financial institutions, a huge research staff that pores over past financial statements, incredible knowledge of industry-specific trends. Yet many of them can't forecast earnings and revenue very accurately. The second reason that trading profitably around earnings announcements is difficult is surprising to many people. Even if you *could* predict earnings surprises and revenue surprises perfectly, this still does not guarantee a profitable trade, because the market reaction often is in the *opposite direction* of the earnings surprise. We conducted an analysis of over 100,000 earnings announcements spanning the last 30 years of publicly traded companies. Our analysis (which we detail in later chapters) shows that about 40% of the time, good earnings news is met with negative market reactions, and bad earnings news is met with positive market reactions. (A prior study that examined a different sample and used different methodologies reported similar findings.) We've all seen the occasional perplexing market reaction, but could you have guessed that this happens 40% of the time? It's no wonder that Bob had such a hard time making money in the market. Even if you predict the right direction of the earnings surprise, you still have a good chance of losing money if you make a directional bet.

So how can an investor profit from an earnings announcement without having to predict the difficult-to-predict earnings-announcement returns? What would Bob have done if he had read this book before putting on his RIMM trade? He would have stayed away from the stock and instead implemented an options-trading strategy called a *straddle*. Specifically, we would have convinced Bob that, although earnings-announcement returns are quite large, they're also extremely difficult to predict. We would have recommended an options position that can be profitable regardless of the direction of the market's reaction to the earnings announcement (as long as the reaction is sufficiently large). Let's talk details.

The Options-Based Trade

Recall that Bob put on a 200-share position of RIMM at $83.06 near market close right before the earnings announcement was made. This represented a $16,612 investment. Instead, we would have recommended purchasing option contracts: buying two put options and two call options, both with an $85 strike price and October 2009 expiration. A call option gives Bob the right, but not the obligation, to buy 100 shares of RIMM at the exercise price of $85. Similarly, a put option gives Bob the right to sell 100 shares of RIMM at $85. So why would Bob purchase both the calls and the puts? Buying the calls and puts simultaneously means that Bob doesn't have to care in which direction the stock price goes. The intuition behind the strategy is straightforward. If RIMM's stock price goes up, Bob's call options increase in value while his put options decrease in value. Alternatively, if RIMM goes down, the puts increase in value while the calls lose value. No matter what happens, Bob will have a profitable trade if the increase in value of one side of his position is more than the decrease in value of the other side.

Let's look at the numbers. When Bob bought shares of RIMM for $83.06, he could have instead bought two puts (with $85 strike price, October 2009 expiration) for the going price of $6.17 each. At the same time, he could have also bought two calls for $4.36 each. Since each option contract's price represents 100 shares, that means an initial investment of $(2 \times 100 \times \$6.17) + (2 \times 100 \times \$4.36) = \$2,106$. We chose to buy two contracts of each because this translates into an initial investment ($2,106) that is close to Bob's loss on his equity trade (−$2,516).

After RIMM's earnings announcement, its stock price declined to $70.48 a share. It turns out that Bob's puts increased in value to a whopping $16.45, while his calls plummeted in value to $0.25 (see Figure 1.2). This translates to a total gain of $2 \times 100 \times (16.45 - 6.17) = \$2,056$ for the put options, and a total loss of $2 \times 100 \times (0.25 - 4.36) = -\$822$ for the call options. Since Bob bought both puts and calls, his net gain is $2,056 − $822 = $1,234.

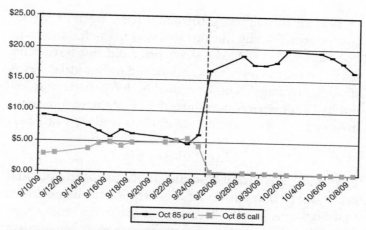

FIGURE 1.2   *RIMM October 85 call and October 85 put prices in the 20 trading days surrounding the earnings announcement*

There are a couple things to note here. First, we avoided Bob's big $2,516 loss. Second, because Bob owned both puts and calls, the gain would have come regardless of whether RIMM's stock had a big move up or a big move down. In the example, because of the big move down in RIMM's price, the increase in the value of Bob's put options overwhelmed the decrease in the value of Bob's call options. If there had instead been a big move up in RIMM's price, the opposite would have happened. Either way, Bob wins. Third, the net gain of $1,234 was made from an initial options investment of only $2,106. That's a 58.6% return on investment in *one day*—without even predicting the *direction* of the stock price movement.

Is it really that easy to make these big returns? Of course not. Trading options involves many hidden risks. For instance, if RIMM's share price did *not* have a big move up or down (but instead moved only a little), Bob's straddle strategy would probably have been unprofitable. Don't worry. We'll inform you of the various risks involved in implementing the options trading strategies.

Our Philosophy

Our main goal is to describe the incredible potential profitability that exists for short-term options positions that are specifically targeted at earnings announcements. To do this, take heart, dear reader, because we do not take the easy way out. We emphasize understanding the theory behind our trades and why we believe in them and discuss findings that have been tested and documented through millions of observations that span decades of research. Once we've built a strong, economically intuitive foundation for our trades, we dive right in to show you real examples of recent profitable trades—as well as trades gone wrong.

Endnote

1. *How concentrated are returns surrounding earnings announcements? For the majority of large-cap stocks, the return over the three trading days surrounding a quarterly earnings announcement is larger than +/-2%. Assuming that the average annual stock market return is about 7%, this 2% earnings-announcement return represents 30% of the total annual return. This 2% return is realized in only 3 trading days, representing just 0.12% of the trading days in a given year.*

Part II

Theory: Earnings Announcements and Earnings Surprises

The chapters in this part cover everything you ever wanted to know about earnings announcements and earnings surprises. **Chapter 2** discusses what earnings announcements are, why they're important, and some of their most important features. **Chapter 3** defines what an earnings surprise is and discusses why even the definition/calculation of an earnings surprise is so rife with ambiguities. **Chapter 4** presents empirical evidence of what earnings surprises look like, including examples of individual companies, as well as examples of large sample sizes spanning 25 years of data on publicly traded companies. We then show you how the pattern of earnings surprises has changed over time.

Chapter 2

Earnings Announcements: Why Are They So Important?

T his chapter discusses how earnings announcements are made, why they're so important, and
some of their critical features. It's important to
understand these basic concepts of earnings announcements because they are the building blocks of the
options trading strategies discussed in later chapters.

What Are Quarterly Earnings Announcements, and Why Are They Important?

In the United States, publicly traded companies are
required by the Securities and Exchange Commission
(SEC) to publicly report their financial performance
each quarter. The formal quarterly reports submitted to
the SEC are called the 10-Q reports. However, most
companies officially announce their quarterly performance numbers weeks before the 10-Q reports are due to
be submitted. Because earnings per share (EPS) is a key
metric in the announcements, these announcements are
generally called *earnings announcements*.

Quarterly earnings announcements are important because they are the most salient, most anticipated *regularly recurring* announcements that companies make. Therefore, they are the most-watched piece of information that comes directly from the source. Many other types of information saturate the marketplace, but no other information source can boast that it regularly and consistently comes from the people who know the business the best.[1] Quarterly earnings announcements also are considered the most *reliable* source of information. This is largely because companies are subject to SEC Rule 10b-5, which provides strict rules about erroneous and/or misleading disclosures. Companies often are sued (under class-action lawsuits) for disclosing information that is construed as misleading. Although exceptions always occur, in the vast majority of cases, this risk of being sued ensures that companies try their best to provide accurate, reliable information. This is why earnings announcements are so salient and important. It is true that information about the company comes from many different places. For instance, the media produces information by publishing news, opinion pieces, and interviews with experts. Financial analysts predict a company's future performance and assess stock value. Indeed, any individual who cares to express his or her opinions about a stock can do so via a blog or message board on the Internet. However, because the strict requirements of SEC Rule 10b-5 apply to only the company, the company's quarterly earnings announcement is considered the most reliable.

How Are Quarterly Earnings Announcements Made?

A typical quarterly earnings announcement proceeds as follows. The company first tells the general public its intended earnings announcement date. After this date is determined, it is not changed unless something unusual happens within the firm. (Indeed, many studies have found that postponing the announcement date usually is a sign of bad news and causes a negative stock price reaction.) For the first three fiscal quarters, the announcement date typically is set 2 to 4 weeks after the fiscal quarter ends. For example, if a company's first fiscal quarter ends in March, earnings for this quarter typically are announced in the 2 to 4 weeks after March 31. However, a company's fourth-quarter earnings announcement usually takes longer, because the annual results (up to and including the fourth quarter) are required to be audited by an independent public accounting firm. The fourth-quarter announcement is made within 3 months after the fiscal quarter ends. So, for a company that has a December 31 fiscal year-end, the fourth quarter results will most likely be announced some time in February or March of the following year. (Because of this lag, there is often only a few weeks' gap between the fourth-quarter and following first-quarter earnings announcement.)

EPS and other performance numbers are released on the earnings announcement date, typically in the form of a press release. (Press releases are most commonly disseminated through Business Wire or PR Newswire.) In addition, the company's management (the CEO,

CFO, and other top executives) usually hosts a conference call that is open to all investors, analysts, the press, and the general public. This conference call typically is scheduled to take place on announcement day or the following day. During the conference call, management discusses the company's financial performance for the past quarter, as well as the company's future challenges and opportunities. Management also typically provides at least some guidance for future quarters' performance. This guidance ranges from being very specific ("We expect EPS to be 22 cents next quarter") to downright murky ("We believe EPS will be flat or higher next quarter"). Of course, the investing community wants as much detailed information as possible—and the Q&A session during the conference call certainly tries to delve into such detailed information. Questions fielded from analysts and investors typically try to shine light on some of the specific details of the earnings announcement just released, as well as further details about its future. Transcripts of the conference calls often are available shortly after the call for those who could not join the call.

Consider the earnings announcement made by JCPenney (NYSE: JCP), a retailer that sells merchandise and services to consumers through its department stores and direct (Internet/catalog) channels. It operates 1,108 JCPenney department stores nationwide. This announcement was made on May 14, 2010, before the market opened, via Business Wire for the first quarter of 2010 ended May 1, 2010.

In the announcement, JCPenney management started by highlighting the quarter's earnings per share, which was $0.25, compared to $0.11 in the same quarter last year. Management attributed the solid improvement in earnings performance to customers' favorable response to its marketing strategies. And although EPS was at the center of the disclosure, it was not the only performance measure that mattered. For instance, because JCPenney operates in the retail industry, investors care a great deal about several other standard performance measures, including comparable store sales, gross margin, and the net number of new stores opened. Not surprisingly, JCPenney management then discussed operating performance in detail by breaking down the performance by business sectors and geographic regions, as well as by individual revenue and expense items. They announced that revenues increased across the board, gross margin expanded, and operating margin improved as well. Next they talked about the company's financial condition, highlighting liquidity and capital expenditure issues. In particular, total cash and short-term investments were $2.4 billion, and long-term debt was $3 billion on May 1, 2010. Capital expenditure for the first quarter was $116 million, as expected. Finally, management provided guidance for the upcoming quarter, as well as for the full 2010 fiscal year. This guidance was in effect a projected income statement because it included practically all the items on a typical income statement, including sales, gross margin, SG&A expenses, depreciation and amortization, interest expense, and the income tax rate. Because it provided insight into how management saw the future of its own company, this guidance was a highly anticipated (but voluntary) part of the discussion. Lastly, management provided details for the three main financial statements of the current quarter: the income statement, the balance sheet, and the statement of cash flows.

Not all companies' earnings announcements are as comprehensive as JCPenney's. Industry practice, the disclosure policies adopted by management, and some other considerations can all influence the richness of information in these earnings announcements. Nonetheless, the JCPenney example demonstrates that earnings announcements are much more than simply earnings per share.

Critical Features of Earnings Announcements

At least six unique features of quarterly earnings announcements make them the center of attention for many investors—and ripe for us to trade options around. We have briefly mentioned some of these features already, but it is worth giving them their full due.

Predictable Timing

First, unlike media coverage or rumors, whose occurrence is inherently unpredictable, quarterly earnings announcement dates are highly predictable and very regular. Many companies follow a predetermined earnings announcement schedule, so the announcement date for the current or upcoming quarter is usually quite close to that of the same quarter last year. In addition, companies typically inform investors of the exact announcement dates at least a week before the actual announcement. Free online earnings calendars allow investors to easily track the earnings announcement dates of thousands of companies. (For instance, the *Wall Street Journal* provides an earnings calendar at http://online.wsj.com/mdc/public/page/ markets_calendar.html.) This predictability makes earnings announcements a perfect candidate for event-driven options-trading strategies. And because they are regularly recurring events, we get four opportunities each year. In comparison, the timing of a merger-and-acquisition announcement or new-product announcement is almost impossible to predict.

Reliability

Second, due to strict regulations (under the Securities Exchange Act of 1934) and severe legal consequences (under SEC Rule 10b-5), the information that management provides in earnings announcements is quite reliable. You may have to read between the lines, but outright lies are extremely rare.

Newsworthiness

Third, the information disclosed in earnings announcements is more or less *new* news to everyone. There was a time when certain people were privy to information before regular investors were, but those times are essentially gone. On August 15, 2000, the SEC adopted a new law called Regulation Fair Disclosure (Reg FD) that prohibits companies from disclosing material information to a select few. Companies are now required to release information to everyone at the same time. That is, they must disclose *fairly*, to everyone. This new law levels the playing field between investment professionals such as financial analysts (who were sometimes leaked important information) and regular retail investors (who were always kept in the dark).

Large Market Movements

The fourth unique feature of earnings announcements arises partially from the features just discussed. Specifically, because the earnings announcement is the most reliable and is less likely to be leaked beforehand, this means that earnings announcements usually are met with larger price reactions when the news is released. (The announcement's reliability is important because if the news isn't credible, there's less chance that the market will respond strongly.) Indeed, as we show in later chapters, both price movements and trading volume around earnings announcements typically are much higher relative to normal, nonannouncement days. Our analysis shows that half of the earnings announcements made by companies have market returns that are *30 times as large* as a typical nonannouncement day. These features make earnings announcements great candidates for options trading—particularly volatility-driven options strategies.

Clustering

The fifth unique feature of earnings announcements is that they do not happen with the same frequency every day, but tend to cluster. This is because many companies have the same fiscal quarter end months. Calendar quarter ends (that is, March 31, June 30, September 30, and December 31) are also the fiscal quarter ends for about 65% of publicly traded companies. Certain industries have their own norms. For example, retailers usually use January 31 as their fiscal year-end. Because the busy holiday season spans November to January, it makes sense to group these months into the same "year." The concentration of fiscal quarter-ends, coupled with the requirement from the SEC to report financial results within a certain number of days, inevitably creates the much-talked-about *earnings seasons*. As a tradition, many market participants use Alcoa's (NYSE: AA) earnings announcement date as the start of an earnings season. They mark the end of the earnings season roughly a month later, because most of the S&P 500 companies have reported their performance by then. The clustering behavior of earnings announcements has important implications for investors for two reasons. One reason is the so-called *confounding effect*. When several companies announce their earnings at the same time, the stock price of one company may react to the news of another company, particularly if the two companies operate within the same industry. Especially in recent times, when risk aversion and investor fear have been running high, the earnings announcements of certain companies have had a large impact on the market as a whole, because these companies' earnings are used as a barometer for general economic conditions. The other reason why clustering is important is that investors have what behavioral finance experts call *limited attention*. Simply put, when there is too much news to digest, investors don't have the time, will, or cognitive ability to fully analyze all the value-relevant implications contained in the news. Consistent with this view, recent research shows that when multiple announcements are clustered in a given day, investors tend to *underreact* to the news; that is, the news is not completely reflected in stock prices. Similarly, investors tend to underreact more to earnings announcements made on Fridays, perhaps because people are distracted by anticipating and planning for upcoming weekend activities or travel.

Other Information Provided

Finally, as the JCPenney example illustrates, earnings announcements contain much more information than simply the EPS number. Research shows that the growing trend among companies over the past decade is to provide ever-expanding disclosures in the announcements, including a detailed income statement, balance sheet, and cash flow information. Investors demanded more information, and they're now getting it. Moreover, management is more likely than before to provide forward-looking information, such as earnings and sales guidance for future quarters, during earnings announcements. Such guidance is not required by law and is done on a strictly voluntary basis. Management also discusses the business environment, opportunities, and risks, and answers questions from investors and analysts. All these additional pieces of disclosure make earnings announcements much more informative than they were even 10 years ago. For investors, the practical implication of all this rich information released with the earnings announcements is that focusing on the earnings number may not be enough. This quarter's EPS is clearly influential, but all the other information—in particular, the forward-looking information—can have a large impact on stock prices as well.

Endnote

1. *Managers also make the occasional voluntary disclosure throughout the year that is outside the scope of the financial statements. These voluntary disclosures can be very informative, but they are still less reliable than the quarterly earnings announcements. For an interesting setting of voluntary disclosures, see Shon and Weiss (2009).*

Chapter 3

Earnings Surprises: Definition and Measurement

In the previous chapter, we discussed why earnings announcements are so important. This chapter defines what an earnings surprise is. On the surface, it sounds straightforward. However, both components of the earnings surprise—the actual earnings and the market's expectations of earnings—are rife with ambiguities that are worth clarifying. The actual earnings and the expected earnings come in different flavors that can affect how we view an earnings surprise. Sometimes, a positive earnings surprise defined in one way turns into a negative earnings surprise when the definition is tweaked.

Definition of an Earnings Surprise

An earnings surprise is the difference between the actual earnings number that is reported by a company's management and what market expectations were. A positive surprise means that the actual earnings are higher than expectations, and a negative surprise means the opposite. For example, if the market's expectation for a company's earnings is $0.20 per share and a company reports $0.22 per share, the earnings surprise is a positive $0.02 per share. On the other hand, if the company reports $0.18 earnings per share, that equals a negative surprise of $0.02 per share. This may sound simple enough, but in reality earnings surprises can be a tricky concept, because neither the actual earnings nor the market's expectations of the earnings are straightforward—or even directly observable.

Actual Earnings: Order of Presentation

For all publicly traded companies, accounting earnings, or net income, reported on an income statement is computed in accordance with generally accepted accounting principles (GAAP). If you've ever read the income statement of a publicly traded company, you will have noted several intermediary steps on the income statement before you get to the bottom-line net income figure. For instance, companies typically report *operating earnings* and *earnings from continuing operations* before getting to *net income*. Without getting into the technical details, generally these various measures of earnings differ from each other because they each represent different perceived notions of *recurrence*. The income statement is presented in a way that emphasizes the probability of each component's recurrence. Items presented near the top of the statement—revenues and expenses such as cost of sales, selling, and general and administrative expenses—have a higher probability of recurring. Conversely, items presented closer to the bottom of the income statement have a lower probability of recurring; this includes things such as special items and extraordinary items. From a user's point of view, this presentation of the income statement makes sense. We want to see components of earnings that we're most likely to see repeatedly, quarter after quarter, near the top. Similarly, we're not as concerned with components of earnings that happened to occur this quarter but that we probably won't see very often. So these types of things are presented near the bottom of the income statement, where they are stressed less. Thus, we will see that *operating earnings*, presented near the top of the income statement, include all revenues and expenses that are deemed to be recurring, but exclude special items or extraordinary items. Meanwhile, further down the income statement, *earnings from continuing operations* include special items but exclude discontinued operations and other extraordinary items. Last, near the very bottom, net income includes everything and hence is called the bottom-line number.

Actual Earnings: Distinction Between GAAP and Street Definitions

With all this talk about a company's actual earnings, it seems natural to think that this net income number is the one that the investing community concentrates on. Not so. The earnings announced by a company's management, discussed in conference calls, and analyzed by the investment community may be completely different from the earnings listed on the income statement. From an investor's standpoint, the main determinant of a stock's value is the portion of earnings that is mostly likely to recur quarter after quarter. This is sometimes called the recurring portion of earnings, or *permanent earnings*. Any one-time, nonrecurring portions of earnings should have limited impact on a stock's value and therefore are relatively unimportant in considering the company's future value-creating capability. For example, during economic downturns, a company may have to lay off some of its employees and incur severance payments to these employees. The market may view such severance payments as a *nonrecurring* expense because a company is not expected to lay off employees on a regular basis. It needs a certain minimum number of employees to function. In this particular example, the market may therefore adjust for the "one-time" severance payment in its computation of actual earnings. If we adopt this logic, we can see why *operating earnings* is the type of measure that investors probably care more about. However, operating earnings are still not the same as the actual earnings recognized by the market. Let's talk about a widely cited study to further illustrate this point.

In a study by Bradshaw and Sloan (2002), the authors compared GAAP earnings with so-called *street earnings*. The authors defined GAAP earnings as the operating earnings reported on a company's income statement, and they defined street earnings to be what Wall Street brokerage firms defined as actual earnings. Street earnings typically were an adjusted version of GAAP earnings and tended to vary across different industries (because different components were added or ignored, depending on the specifics of each industry).

What the authors found in this comparison was that there were significant differences between GAAP earnings versus street earnings. This was despite the fact that both measures attempt to measure the same thing: a company's accounting performance. Moreover, they found that over time, the difference between the two measures was increasing. This suggests that investors (or, more accurately, Wall Street analysts) seem to disagree more and more with standard GAAP earnings as time marches on. Perhaps most interestingly, the study also found that street earnings were usually *better* (that is, more positive) than GAAP earnings at capturing the companies' true economic performance. This suggests that analysts believed that, on average, standard accounting practice as laid out in GAAP understated companies' true earnings power. This view has some truth. For example, research-and-development expenditures are treated as expenses under GAAP, but most would argue that in a knowledge-based economy, treating such expenditures as investments or assets may be more appropriate. If investors were to redo the accounting with respect to research-and-development expenditures, the earnings they calculated would be higher than earnings calculated using GAAP. Similarly, another study by Brown and Sivakumar (2003) found that the street earnings were more value-relevant than GAAP earnings. Consistent with these types of findings, nowadays many companies, especially those with more knowledge-based assets such as software and biotech companies, tend to issue *pro forma* earnings along with their GAAP earnings. Pro forma earnings are meant to modify standard accounting treatment to more accurately reflect the "true" earnings of such companies.

What is interesting (and perhaps unsurprising) is that the pro forma earnings also tend to be better than GAAP earnings.

This discussion suggests that GAAP seems to underestimate a company's "true" earnings, and that Wall Street—analysts, investors, and even the companies themselves—has been making quick fixes to these earnings (calling them street earnings or pro forma earnings) to bring them closer to reality. From the sounds of it, this pleads the case for a major revamp of GAAP. But let's try to remain objective here. On the other hand, it's also possible that Wall Street analysts and corporate management are intentionally overstating earnings because they have an inherent bias to be bullish. After all, all these parties win (at least in the short run) when earnings are higher and stock prices increase. So which is it? Are street earnings better? Or are they worse? Some studies have examined this issue, but the evidence is mixed. On the one hand, a study by Doyle, Lundholm, and Soliman (2003) found that the difference between GAAP earnings and pro forma earnings— the so-called *nonrecurring* component of earnings—is in fact important and seems to be priced by the market in a way that suggests that it is more recurring than the Street thinks. (Indeed, the authors detail how you can earn abnormal stock returns by exploiting the differences between the two earnings.) On the other hand, a study by Chen and Gu (2004) found that analysts exhibit good judgment in deciding which nonrecurring items to include and exclude from street earnings. Specifically, the authors found that the nonrecurring items analysts decide to keep in street earnings are more persistent/recurring that those they exclude. Moreover, they found no value-relevant information in the items that were excluded that would help predict future stock returns. This suggests that the Street *does* seem to make good judgments on the recurring portions of earnings.

In the end, because the studies found almost opposite results, for our purposes the jury is still out. However, we wanted to describe both sides of the argument so that you would be aware of these thorny issues when ultimately judging the validity of earnings surprises. Was the earnings surprise positive or negative? Was it based on GAAP or street earnings? These are important questions to answer in forming a final conclusion about the nature of the surprise. Moreover, there's no reason to think so black-and-white about this issue. It's possible that both sides are (partially) correct. Perhaps faulty GAAP and overly optimistic analysts/managers both contribute to the difference between GAAP and street earnings. Whatever the reasons, it's clear that defining even actual earnings isn't a straightforward task. Going back to the JCPenney example from Chapter 2, "Earnings Announcements: Why Are They So Important?" even if an investor knew in advance that the company was planning to report earnings of $0.25 per share, it's not clear whether the components included in the announced earnings number are the same as those included in the market's expected numbers.

Earnings Management

The last point we want to briefly mention about actual earnings is the issue of *earnings management*. Companies engage in earnings management to meet or beat market expectations because the consequence of missing expectations is severe. It's not news to state that accounting earnings are subject to potential earnings management. On September 28, 1998, former SEC chairman Arthur Levitt delivered a now-famous speech titled "The Numbers Game." In the speech, Mr. Levitt outlined five common accounting practices that managers engage in to manipulate earnings: big bath charges, creative acquisition accounting, miscellaneous cookie jar reserves, materiality, and revenue recognition. Although this topic is beyond the scope of this book, countless studies have found evidence suggesting that earnings management is alive and well in the markets. However, it isn't quite clear how this (potentially) pervasive earnings management actually plays out in the market. If it's that pervasive, financial analysts and the market itself would adjust their expectations for such earnings management, making it a true numbers game that is played dynamically and simultaneously by both sides. It's important to stress here that earnings management is not always a significant, headline-grabbing, gigantic amount that eventually brings a company to its knees. More often than not, earnings management takes place in smaller amounts that go forever unnoticed, increasing earnings by a penny in one year, decreasing it by a penny the following year. And although the occasional discovery of earnings management reported in the press can have significant long-run implications for the company's present and future operations, the short-run implications are much more difficult to assess. After all, earnings management cannot be immediately determined from an *earnings announcement*. Discovering such earnings management takes long, steady detective work; a team of forensic accountants; and a cadre of tax attorneys. Thus, earnings management is not a significant issue for the trading strategies discussed in this book.

Expected Earnings: The Benchmark

The other leg of the earnings surprise calculation, the market's earnings expectation, is perhaps even more difficult to gauge than the actual earnings. Different investors may have different expectations with respect to a particular company's earnings, but the market's expectation is not the simple average of all the individual investors' expectations. After all, would you place the same importance on the expectations of your grandmother (who doesn't know a revenue from an expense) as the expectations of a star analyst who has been following a company for 20 years? It's safe to say that you place greater value on the analyst's opinion. Similarly, you should value the expectations of active, short-term investors over those of passive, long-term investors, because short-term investors trade more often and therefore affect short-term price movements more. (Conversely, long-term investors typically buy and hold over a long period and therefore care much less about any particular quarter's earnings.) Thus, to form the market's true expectations about a company's earnings, we need to know the individual expectation of every investor in the market, as well as the optimal weight that we should put on each person's expectations. This is obviously an impossible task.

Expectations Based on Time Series

It's clear that the true market expectation is unobservable. But we can try to use the observable information that is available to us to estimate it. We can do this in two ways. The first approach is to assume that investors estimate future earnings using *time-series* models. A time-series model is a statistical model that aims to analyze data points over time. The simplest time-series model is a *random-walk* model, which simply states that this quarter's earnings are expected to be the same as last quarter's earnings. That is, the market's expectations for earnings are simply what they were the last time we checked. This model, although extremely simple, performs reasonably well. However, it generates very large forecast errors when applied to businesses with strong seasonality. For instance, retailers generate a significant portion of their earnings in the holiday season, so clearly the holiday-season quarter's earnings are very different from other quarters' earnings. This example suggests that quarterly earnings may follow a *seasonal* random walk, which means that this quarter's earnings are expected to equal those of the same quarter from last year. This is certainly a tweak to the time series model that makes intuitive sense. Therefore, perhaps a seasonal random-walk model gives us a good approximation of what the market expects earnings of, say, JCPenney to be. A further tweak of the model would allow the expectations to include some room for companies to grow (or *drift*). After all, it's a bit unrealistic to say that earnings will be the same as the prior quarter for a company that has been growing exponentially. The point is that time-series models can handle such complexities. The most significant issue with a time-series model such as the random-walk model is that we are assuming that the market forms its expectations of earnings by using a fairly simple formula. If this is true, the key to success is in determining the right formula. With that said, prior studies have found that time-series models seem to do a fairly decent job of forecasting future earnings.

Expectations Based on Analysts' Consensus Forecasts

The second, alternative (and superior) way to estimate earnings expectations is to use financial analysts' earnings forecasts. Sell-side financial analysts are important information intermediaries in the financial markets.[1] Analysts expend significant time, skills, and resources to excavate as much information as possible about the companies they follow. The information they gather and process includes public information, the most important of which is the company's financial statements and the footnotes that accompany them. Analysts pore through a wealth of information in these footnotes to gain insight into the company's inner workings. Their ultimate goal is to construct the most precise estimate they can of the company's future earnings. Along with these financial statements, analysts study other inputs, including analysis of time-series models, as well as proprietary valuation models developed internally. Last, if the company itself has provided earnings guidance, obviously this is an extremely important input into the analyst's own earnings forecast. Given the effort and additional information that is gathered by these financial analysts, it is not surprising to hear that researchers have examined the performance of these analysts' earnings forecasts relative to simple times-series models. Overall, these studies have found that analysts' forecasts are far from perfect, but collectively, the forecasts do a pretty good job.

Analyst following or coverage varies greatly. Many companies are quite small and illiquid and are not followed by any analysts. At the other end of the spectrum, some companies are followed by numerous analysts. For example, Apple Inc. (NASDAQ: AAPL) is followed by 47 analysts, Exxon Mobile Corp. (NYSE: XOM) is followed by 21 analysts, and Microsoft Corporation (NASDAQ: MSFT) is followed by 34 analysts. When more than one analyst makes a forecast, the market uses a *consensus earnings forecast* to proxy for the unobservable *market expectation.* The consensus forecast typically is the average or median of all the analysts' forecasts made over a certain period, such as 30 days. More sophisticated models place different weights on different analysts' forecasts.[2] The consensus forecast provides a practical solution in approximating the market's expectations of a company's future earnings and therefore is the most widely used measure. These consensus forecasts are available from many public websites, such as Yahoo! Finance.

Let's discuss Home Depot (NYSE: HD) as an example. About 25 analysts issue earnings forecasts for Home Depot. In the July 2010 quarter, the average earnings forecast among all the estimates for the upcoming quarter was $0.71 per share. This average is composed of estimates that range from a high of $0.74 to a low of $0.68. Among these estimates may be those coming from fairly novice analysts who are employed by small brokerage houses, to experienced analysts employed by major bulge-bracket investment houses with a very good track record of forecasting Home Depot's earnings. Regardless of the profiles of the individual analysts who make up this consensus, the point is that some *divergence of opinion* exists among professionals. Higher divergence or dispersion in the estimates suggests a higher level of uncertainty about the company. Home Depot has a $0.06 range in estimates (from $0.68 to $0.74), which is a fairly tight range. Contrast this with a company such as Bank of America (NYSE: BAC). Its most recent consensus estimate was $0.18 but ranged as high as $0.33 and as low as $0.01. Such companies have a very high level of divergence.[3] Last, forecasts typically are provided for past and future periods as well. For instance, for Home Depot, last year's EPS is also provided, which is what you want to know if you are implicitly assuming a time-series, random-walk model. For Home Depot, last year's EPS was $0.64. Also, the forecasts for the following quarter, October 2010, are provided, as well as those for the full fiscal years ending January 2011 and January 2012.

The computation of consensus analyst forecasts is not without problems. First, not all analysts issue their forecasts at the same time. This means that some forecasts are timelier than others. It is intuitive to place more weight on more timely, recent forecasts than on older, stale ones that do not incorporate the latest news. Indeed, countless studies have shown that a forecast's timeliness (or *forecast horizon*) is *the* dominant factor in determining forecast accuracy. The last, most recent forecast made usually is more accurate than the consensus forecast. This makes sense, because the last person to make a forecast has access to what the consensus is up to that point. From there he can also incorporate any new information into his forecast. Second, analysts can use different definitions of earnings. As we discussed earlier, different analysts may decide to include or exclude different items in their earnings forecasts. If we take a simple average of forecasts made by different analysts without knowing exactly what their definitions of earnings are, we may be comparing apples to oranges.

Earnings Guidance: How Managers Affect Both Actual and Expected Earnings

Earlier, we briefly discussed earnings management and how managers manipulate actual earnings in an attempt to meet or beat market expectations. In a similar vein, it's also possible for managers to manipulate *expected* earnings. Specifically, the market's expectations of earnings are a function of the individual analysts' forecasts. Therefore, managers may try to manipulate analysts' forecasts. Several studies have found that managers and analysts engage in a two-way *earnings guidance* game. Managers use the power of their earnings guidance to gradually "walk down" analysts' forecasts to a beatable level. They do this by making public statements that subtly bring down the expectations of analysts, discouraging overly optimistic forecasts while corroborating more down-to-earth forecasts.[4] The findings show a clear pattern of analysts' forecast revisions that is consistent with this earnings guidance game. Specifically, analysts tend to issue optimistic forecasts at the beginning of each period, but as time progresses, they gradually revise their earnings forecasts downward. By the time actual earnings are officially announced, the consensus forecasts may be below the actual earnings that management announces. This suggests that, *on average*, earnings surprises are predictably positive. However, it is still difficult to predict *which* company's earnings surprises will be positive. In theory, you could try to investigate such possibilities by examining the statements that companies are making and try to connect them to downward revisions that analysts subsequently make, but this is not easy. Moreover, given the fact that investors are also aware of this guidance game, even if we could predict the companies that would have positive earnings surprises, that wouldn't necessarily be met with a positive market reaction.

Endnotes

1. Sell-side analysts attempt to sell their services (typically in the form of analyst reports and advice) to potential investors. On the other hand, buy-side analysts analyze companies for the purposes of investing for their own proprietary accounts, such as hedge funds.

2. *Some analysts have a better reputation than others, perhaps because they've demonstrated that they have superior abilities in forecasting earnings or recommending profitable trades. Should an analyst's reputation matter? In other words, does an analyst who exhibits superior earnings forecasting ability in the past continue to make more accurate forecasts in the future? The answer is yes. Brown (2001) found that an analyst's past forecast accuracy is the most important predictor of future forecast accuracy. This pleads the case that better analysts should be given more weight or emphasis in calculating market expectations. In the extreme (although we do not recommend it), you may simply use the forecast of the one "star" analyst as what you believe the market expects for earnings. Park and Stice (2000) found that the forecast revisions of star analysts generate larger market reactions. However, this reputation doesn't seem to carry over to the other firms that the star analyst covers. In another study, Bonner, Hugon, and Walther (2007) found that investors react more strongly to the forecast revisions of "celebrity" analysts that are more widely covered by the media, even though these analysts didn't seem to forecast more accurately than their less-media-covered peers.*

3. *How does this uncertainty affect stock valuation? Miller (1977) put forth a theory that stocks with more uncertainty tend to be overvalued because of short-selling constraints. Diether, Malloy, and Scherbina (2002) used analysts' forecast dispersion (the standard deviation of forecasts) to measure divergence of opinions. They found that, consistent with Miller's prediction, stocks with high forecast dispersion tend to earn lower returns. Chapter 15, "Other Theories and Evidence," discusses the impact of divergence of opinions on earnings announcement returns.*

4. *These voluntary disclosures can have a significant impact on stock prices (and vice versa). See Shon (2009).*

Chapter 4

Earnings Surprises: Empirical Evidence

In the preceding chapter, we discussed many of the difficulties that arise when trying to define and measure the concept of an earnings surprise. On the surface this is a simple endeavor, but in reality it's rife with ambiguities. In this chapter, we conduct original research by gathering the actual earnings surprises of the largest 1,000 publicly traded companies over a 25-year span. We examine the nature of these earning surprises—in particular, their cross-sectional distribution. We also examine how earnings surprises have *changed over time* by examining the time-series trend in these surprises over the past 100 quarters. Overall, the empirical evidence sheds light on the significant role that earnings play even in today's world, where analysts and the general public have access to so much information. But first, we discuss some examples of earnings surprises for a few individual companies.

Individual Examples of Earnings Surprises: AAPL, BAC, and F

We start the chapter with some simple examples of earnings surprises. Several free sources exist for doing research on earnings surprises. For instance, Yahoo! Finance provides free earnings surprise information for the past four quarters (which it receives from Thomson Financial Network; Yahoo! does not calculate such information). You can find the information by entering a company's ticker information into the search bar at http://finance. yahoo.com and then clicking the Analyst Estimates link in the left margin of the company's main page. Similar information can be found on other Internet sites such as the *Wall Street Journal*. Premium, paid information providers such as Thomson Reuters provide much more recent, comprehensive, and granular information.

Let's consider the earnings surprise history of three large companies: Apple (NASDAQ: AAPL), Bank of America (NYSE: BAC), and Ford Motor Company (NYSE: F). Earnings surprises typically are composed of the actual EPS and the estimated (forecast) EPS, and the calculated difference between the two. That calculated difference is the earnings surprise. It is also sometimes calculated as a percentage of the forecast itself.

Earnings surprises can be significant—even for large, well-known companies. Given the wealth of information that is out there for these companies, and the number of resources that analysts invest in forecasting the earnings of these large, blue-chip companies, you would think that the surprises for such well-followed stocks would be fairly small. But this is not the case. For instance, for Ford, the forecast EPS for September 2009 was –$0.12, but its actual EPS was $0.26, a difference of $0.38—or a 316.7% surprise! Depending on your prior beliefs, even 20% surprises could be interpreted as fairly large. For instance, Bank of America's forecast EPS for June 2010 was $0.22, but its actual EPS was reported as $0.27. This is a $0.05 difference, or 22.7% surprise. You might think that this is simply a function of choosing earnings surprises during the tumultuous 2009–2010 period, but we show you evidence that earnings surprises are quite large even in normal market conditions. These large earnings surprises reinforce the conclusions from the preceding chapter: It is extremely difficult to accurately forecast earnings.

Another pattern that emerges from examining some companies is that analysts seem to persistently issue *biased* forecasts. For example, both Apple and Ford had four consecutive quarters of large positive earnings surprises. For the past four quarters (starting in September 2009), Apple's earnings surprises were 95.1%, 75.6%, 35.9%, and 12.5%—all very positive. Ford's past four quarters also have been consistently positive; earnings surprises were 316.7%, 65.4%, 48.4%, and 70.0%. Are analysts consistently duped? Are biases inherent in their forecasting process?[1] Can we glean anything from this apparent pattern? For instance, are earnings surprises *persistent* over time? (Short answer: Yes. We discuss this issue in Chapter 14, "Earnings Surprise Persistence.") These are all valid questions that arise from a casual perusal of the tables. But they are also questions that will arise when we examine the empirical evidence across a whole spectrum of thousands of company/quarter observations.

Last, a technical note: It is important to note that you should interpret percentage surprise calculations with a fair bit of caution. Percentage surprise calculations (any percentage calculations, for that matter) are sensitive to what is referred to as the *denominator effect*. Essentially, percentages can look quite large simply because the denominator—here, the EPS estimate—is so small. For instance, in the quarter ended March 2010, Bank of America reported a positive earnings surprise of 211.10%. However, this very large earnings

surprise is mainly driven by the close-to-zero EPS estimate of $0.09. Another issue is that EPS estimates can
be negative, and ratios over negative numbers are not
very meaningful. For example, Ford experienced a
316.70% positive earnings surprise in the quarter ended
September 2009. A closer examination shows that the
EPS estimate was a negative number, –$0.12, but the
actual EPS was a positive number, $0.26. If the EPS esti-
mate were –$0.22, the difference would be $0.48, larger
than the $0.38 actual difference, but the calculated per-
centage surprise was only 218.18%, less than 316.70%.

Empirical Evidence Across Companies

Let's now take a look at some large sample evidence of
earnings surprises. It will help us assess the true distribution of earnings surprises across a broad spectrum of
companies, not just the three companies that we ran-
domly chose in the preceding section. To construct a true
representative sample, we restrict our analysis to the large
cap stocks in the Russell 1000 index (that is, the largest
1,000 publicly traded companies in the U.S.). We define
an earnings surprise as the difference between reported
EPS and the median analyst EPS forecast in the 30 days
leading up to each company's earnings announcement.
(We use the median analyst forecast instead of the mean
because the mean can be heavily influenced by very large
or small outlier forecasts. However, our results and conclusions do not change when we do use the mean.) Our
sample period is from 1984 to 2009 and includes a total
of 82,507 earnings surprises during the period.

Because directly comparing earnings surprises in dollar
terms across companies is not meaningful, we need to normalize earnings surprises before we can compare them.

We choose two variables to do this. The first is what Yahoo! Finance uses: the EPS forecast. However, as discussed earlier, this variable suffers from the critical problem that EPS often can be negative or close to zero, making the surprise ratio less meaningful. The second variable we use to normalize earnings surprises is the company's own stock price. This normalization process using stock price is the common standard in academic studies.

Table 4.1 reports the distribution of normalized quarterly earnings surprises for Russell 1000 stocks from July 1984 to December 2009.

TABLE 4.1   *Distribution of Normalized Earnings Surprises*

Distribution	Earnings Surprise Normalized by Consensus EPS Estimate	Earnings Surprise Normalized by Stock Price
Maximum	167.0000	2.1747
90th percentile	0.2564	0.0034
75th percentile	0.0943	0.0013
50th percentile (median)	0.0069	0.0001
25th percentile	−0.0441	−0.0007
10th percentile	−0.2500	−0.0041
Minimum	−479.0000	−9.9601
Mean	−0.0749	−0.0017

The bottom row of Table 4.1 shows that on average the quarterly earnings surprise was −0.0749, or −7.49%, of the consensus analyst EPS estimate. When normalized by stock price, it was −0.0017, or −0.17%, of the stock price. Next, examining the median (50th percentile) surprise, we note that more than half of the earnings surprises were positive. When the consensus EPS estimate is used to normalize earnings surprises, the minimum and maximum normalized earnings surprises were extremely large (167% for the maximum and

–479% for the minimum). This is because the consensus EPS estimates in these cases were very close to zero, creating the *denominator effect* discussed earlier.

Last, we note that many companies experienced relatively large earnings surprises. We can see this from examining the quartile cutoffs. Specifically, the 75th percentile is 9.43%, suggesting that the top 25% of all earnings surprises during this period were larger than 9.43%. Similarly, the 25th percentile is –4.41%, suggesting that the bottom 25% of all earnings surprises during this same period were more negative than –4.41%. These are very large price moves.

The main takeaway from this empirical evidence is that a significant number of earnings surprises spanning the last 25 years have been quite large. This is good news for us, because these large earnings surprises allude to large stock price reactions. And the presence of these large price movements is one of the key ingredients of the trading strategies discussed later.

Empirical Evidence Across Time

How has the distribution of earnings surprises changed over time? One theory is that the abundance of information that is available in recent times, the steady increase in required disclosures that companies are subject to, and the increased talent and resources of sell-side analysts almost guarantee that fewer surprises should occur when earnings are announced. However, the facts, presented in Figure 4.1, do not support this view.

Figure 4.1 shows the percentage of positive, zero, and negative earnings surprises by year. By definition, the total for all three types of surprises equals 100%. Our data starts in 1984 and ends in 2009.

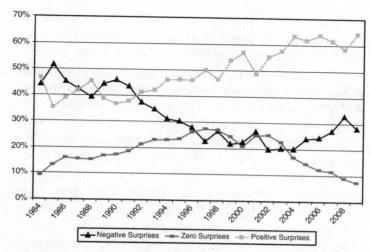

FIGURE 4.1 *Distribution of positive, zero, and negative earnings surprises over time*

Interestingly, we find that over the last 25 years, the percentage of zero earnings surprises—earnings announcements that just meet expectations (that is, *no* surprise)—was fairly steady up until the early 2000s. Since that time, a fairly steady decline has occurred. By definition, this recent decline in zero surprises means that positive and negative earnings surprises have become more common. And that is precisely what we see. Specifically, over the years, we notice a steady decline in negative earnings surprises and a steady increase in positive earnings surprises. This pattern is consistent with the walk-down earnings guidance game we discussed at the end of the preceding chapter. That is, as time goes by, managers are becoming more adept at managing expectations downward so that they can pleasantly surprise the market when they announce earnings. This causes the steady decline in negative earnings surprises and the steady increase in positive ones. However, you'll notice that some of these trends have reversed in the last few years. For instance, the sharp increase in negative earnings surprises and sharp decrease in positive earnings surprises in 2008 reflect the fact that analysts significantly underestimated the severity of the financial crisis. As the economy gradually recovers, we expect to see more positive surprises and fewer negative surprises. This is true because analysts may focus on the dismal performance of companies in the recession and underestimate the strength of the recovery. Indeed, the first two earnings seasons in 2010 saw the majority of companies surprise investors on the upside.

Overall, the main takeaway from this time-series investigation is that, if anything, despite the abundance of information that is out there, earnings surprises seem to be more common than even 5 years ago. Taken together, the evidence in Table 4.1 and Figure 4.1 suggests that earnings surprises can be quite large and that such surprises are not a dying breed. This conclusion is the first step in our thesis on how earnings-announcement-based options trades have the potential to be very profitable. In Part III, we discuss the next step in our thesis—that market reactions to these earnings surprises can be just as large, but also very unpredictable.

Endnote

1. *Many studies document analysts' tendency to issue optimistic forecasts (such as Fried and Givoly, 1982; O'Brien, 1988; and Francis and Philbrick (1993). We discuss these issues—along with other types of analyst biases—in Chapter 15, "Other Theories and Evidence."*

Part III

Evidence:
Market Reactions

Part II discussed the ins and outs of earnings announcements and earnings surprises. Part III talks about the market reactions to these earnings-related events. Market reactions essentially are the stock price movements that occur during the short amount of time around a company's earnings announcement date. **Chapter 5** presents empirical evidence of the market reactions to earnings announcements in general, both across companies and across time. **Chapter 6** presents similar evidence of the market reactions, but this time based on the *direction* of earnings surprises in particular. Only by understanding the movements of the underlying equity securities can you fully appreciate the options-based trading strategies presented in later chapters. Therefore, the next two chapters are essential building blocks of the intellectual development of our options strategies. You also might encounter a few surprises, no matter how closely you follow the markets.

Chapter 5

Market Reactions to Earnings Announcements

In the previous chapters, we talked about earnings announcements (Chapter 2) and earnings surprises (Chapters 3 and 4). In this chapter, we begin our overall discussion of stock price reactions to these earnings-related events. In particular, much like Chapter 4, where we presented evidence on the distribution of earnings surprises, in this chapter, we perform similar empirical tests to show you what the distribution of the market reactions to earnings announcements looks like. Our tests in this chapter look at market reactions without considering the *direction* of the earnings surprise (which we consider in the next chapter). Overall, we find that even in today's world of information overload, market reactions to earnings announcements have actually been increasing in recent years.

What Causes Market Reactions?

As we discussed in prior chapters, earnings announcements contain a great deal of value-relevant information about a company's past, current, and future performance. Let's now take a moment to talk about stock price reactions, or market reactions. Because only new and *unexpected* information should move a company's stock price, an earnings announcement per se does not guarantee a large market reaction. Put differently, to the extent that earnings announcements do not communicate any new information, but only confirm information that the market already knows, the market should not react strongly, because old news is already embedded in stock prices.[1] To the extent that the market *does* seem to react to a relatively uninformative earnings announcement, we must conclude that investors are digesting the information and interpreting bits and pieces of the announcement and coming to conclusions that change their view of the stock price. A certain proportion of speculative traders, day traders, and even some high-frequency traders also might contribute to price movements. Let's leave the underlying reasons for the market reactions aside and take some time to simply examine what these market reactions look like.

Empirical Evidence Across Companies

Our goal in this chapter is to examine a sample of companies and, from the examination, to try to draw inferences about companies *in general*. To do this, we want to create a broad, *representative* sample of the companies we'll be trading in, not some cherry-picked sample of a few companies that help illustrate a preconceived argument. To construct a truly representative sample, we again focus our analysis on all the large-cap stocks in the Russell 1000 index from 1984 to 2009. Our sample includes a total of 110,495 market-reaction observations, representing all the earnings announcements made by the top 1,000 firms during the period.

Table 5.1 shows the distribution of stock market reactions to earnings announcements over the entire 26-year period. The returns we report are *market-adjusted* or *excess* returns, meaning that we subtract the corresponding (value-weighted) market returns from each company's raw returns. This adjustment is used to remove the impact of general market movements and to better isolate the returns that the specific company is experiencing above and beyond general market movements/returns. For instance, suppose the returns during the earnings announcement period for, say, Apple were 3%, and the returns for the S&P 500 during the same period also were 3%. You would have a difficult time saying that Apple had very good announcement period returns, because it had the same returns that any average company had on that day.

Also, to enable you to examine differences in returns over different holding periods, we examine two earnings announcement return windows: a 3-day window return and a 21-day window return. If we denote the earnings announcement date as day 0, the 3-day window return is the return of holding the stock for day −1, day 0, and day +1, where each day is a trading day. The reason we start the calculation one day before the actual announcement and end the calculation one day after the announcement is that earnings can be announced either before the market opens, during regular trading hours, or after the market closes. Starting the return calculation one day early allows for some sense of information leakage that can take place in the immediate time before an earnings announcement. Similarly, ending the return calculation one day later allows ample time for the market to fully digest any of the information. Next, the 21-day window spans from day −19 to day +1. We use a longer window because many companies issue pre-earnings announcements in the days and weeks before their actual earnings announcement, and we want to ensure that we are capturing this special type of information leakage that may be affecting stock prices. Enough details. Let's get to some of the results.

TABLE 5.1   *Distribution of Earnings-Announcement Excess Returns of Russell 1000 Stocks from 1984 to 2009*

Distribution	3-Day Window Return	21-Day Window Return
Maximum	246.24%	332.34%
90th percentile	17.41%	11.57%
75th percentile	2.74%	5.37%
50th percentile (median)	0.10%	0.00%
25th percentile	−2.34%	−5.16%
10th percentile	−5.59%	−10.82%
Minimum	−84.24%	−93.38%
Mean	0.20%	0.31%

Table 5.1 contains several important messages. First, overall, for all the earnings announcement returns spanning the full 26 years, there were about as many positive earnings announcement returns as negative ones. We can conclude this because the median (50th percentile) announcement return was 10 basis points for the 3-day window and 1 basis point for the 21-day window—essentially, about zero. This suggests that half the returns were greater than zero and the other half were less than zero. Next, we look at the average announcement return (presented in the bottom row). Coming in at 20 basis points for the 3-day window returns and 31 basis points for the 21-day window returns, we conclude that, on *average*, earnings announcement returns were not that large.

However, it would be a *huge* mistake to conclude from these numbers that the market reactions to earnings announcements were always small. After all, the average is just that: an average. It doesn't tell us much about the variation in the returns. To examine this, consider the quartile cutoffs. Specifically, for the 3-day window, the 75th percentile return was 2.74%, and the 25th percentile return was –2.34%. This means that 25% of the earnings announcements had returns that were greater than 2.74%, and similarly, 25% of the earnings announcements had returns that were more negative than –2.34%. Over the 21-day window, the corresponding numbers were more than twice as large at 5.37% and –5.16%, respectively. These returns are enormous when compared to the returns during a typical 3-day (or 21-day) time period where no earnings are announced. For instance, assume that, over the past 50 years, the average stock market return was about 7% a year. Also assume that there are roughly 250 trading days per year. On average, that means the daily market return is about 2.8 basis points (=0.07/250). This means that a typical 3-day return is about 8.4 basis points and a typical 21-day return is about 58.8 basis points. Wow. Those are pretty small numbers. When we compare these typical days with those of earnings announcement days, the conclusion is quite stark. It turns out that 50% of the 3-day earnings announcement returns (those above the 75th percentile and below the 25th percentile) are about *30 times* the size of a typical 3-day return and about *10 times* the size of a typical 21-day return. If we examine the announcement returns in the 90th and 10th percentiles, the size of the returns is obviously even more significant. The general conclusion is that market movements during earnings announcement periods can be quite large. (And although it's beyond the scope of this book, similar evidence exists for trading volume and returns volatility.)[2]

Empirical Evidence Across Time

The evidence just discussed suggests that a significant number of earnings announcements were met by very large market reactions when compared to a typical nonannouncement day. However, maybe this phenomenon is just a figment of the past. Do such large market reactions still occur today in the age of information overload? Do such large reactions still occur when so many sophisticated market players have so many technological resources to throw at their trading endeavors? Have market reactions to earnings announcements become less significant over the years? From our analysis, the answer seems to be a resounding no. If anything, earnings announcement returns seem to be even more volatile in recent years. Let's look at the details in the next two figures.

Figure 5.1 shows the 10th, 25th, 75th, and 90th percentile 3-day window earnings announcement returns for *each year* from 1984 to 2009. Figure 5.2 shows the same statistics for the 21-day window. Both figures present an increasing trend in the percentile returns over the 26-year span. For instance, the 90th percentile announcement-period returns start out at a hair less than 5.0% in 1984 but then steadily increase to approximately 12% in 2009. You can make similar conclusions by examining any of the time series in the figures. For instance, the 25th percentile starts in 1984 at approximately –2.5% but ends at about –4.5% in 2009. Quite naturally, in years with elevated market volatility, such as 2000, 2001, 2008, and 2009, the magnitude of earnings announcement returns also increases. However, even if we ignore these years, the conclusion is the same: Market reactions to earnings announcements seem to be increasing in size and intensity as time marches on. Several reasons exist for why this increasing-market-reaction trend is taking place, but they are beyond the scope of this book. What's more important and relevant for us here is that the evidence clearly suggests that the opportunities to profit from options-based trades around earnings announcements have not diminished over the years. Indeed, as market reactions become more volatile, trading opportunities in recent years have become all the more lucrative.

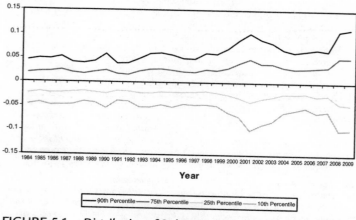

FIGURE 5.1   *Distribution of 3-day earnings-announcement excess returns by year*

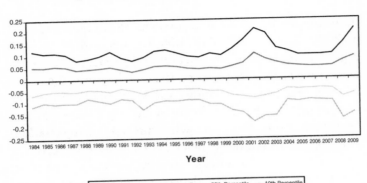

Year

| 90th Percentile | 75th Percentile | 25th Percentile | 10th Percentile |

FIGURE 5.2 *Distribution of 21-day earnings-announcement excess returns by year*

Endnotes

1. *How much does the market know about information in an upcoming earnings announcement? In a famous study published over 40 years, Ball and Brown (1968) found that stock prices tended to steadily run up several months before good earnings numbers were actually reported, and prices tended to steadily trail downward several months before bad earnings were announced. This finding should not be that surprising. The market is incredibly adept at sniffing out information in obscure corners of the world. That's because the market is composed of a host of different types of participants—investors, analysts, employees, suppliers, lenders—who spend time and resources trying to gather information to stay ahead of the game. They gather and analyze historical numbers from past financial statements, visit the company, and talk to many key players, such as management, employees, and competitors. Of course, this sounds a bit contradictory to the evidence that we present in these chapters about the large number of earnings surprises. We promise to clear up the confusion in Chapter 15, "Other Theories and Evidence."*

2. *The market's reaction to earnings announcements is reflected not only in the magnitude of stock returns, but also in the stock's trading volume and return volatility. A pioneer study by Beaver (1968) showed that both trading volume and return volatility spiked during earnings announcement periods. More recently, Landsman and Maydew (2002) confirmed Beaver's results using more recent data and more sophisticated statistical techniques. Their findings run counter to the conjecture that accounting numbers (and earnings announcements) have lost their informativeness due to their alleged lack of reflecting the economics of today's modern companies. Indeed, the authors showed that, if anything, the trading volume and volatility spikes during earnings announcements seemed to become stronger in recent years. (This might be due to the expanded disclosure and earnings guidance found in recent earnings announcements.)*

Chapter 6

Market Reactions to Earnings Surprises (Are Full of Surprises)

In many ways, we consider this chapter to be the *intellectual and theoretical heart* of our book. In the previous chapter, we examined the market reactions to earnings announcements without considering the actual content of the announcements. In other words, did a positive or negative earnings surprise occur? This chapter investigates market reactions considering this directional aspect of earnings surprises. We think you'll find the results quite surprising. What we find is that *almost half* of all earnings surprises are met with market reactions that go in the *opposite* direction. Sure, we've all noticed the occasional positive earnings surprise that the market then punished with a negative stock price reaction. But we don't think anyone could have guessed that this was so common, representing almost every other announcement. The findings we present here really are the backbone of our main options-trading strategies, so it's important that you are fully convinced. Let's talk about the details.

Empirical Evidence Across Companies

We begin with what would probably be viewed as a fairly benign statement about the perceived relationship between earnings surprises and the market reactions to them: In general, the market reacts positively to positive earnings surprises and negatively to negative earnings surprises. Sure, we can cherry-pick a few examples where the opposite is true. But can we make any general, overarching statements about the nature of these market reactions over the past 30 years? Surely, when we consider the broad market as a whole, stock price reactions go in the same direction as earnings surprises, right? Let's get to the empirical evidence.

First, the setup. Our sample is the same as the one used in the previous chapters: the large-cap stocks that comprise the Russell 1000 index, over the period between 1984 and 2009. We define an earnings surprise as the difference between the EPS that the company announces and the EPS that the market was expecting. We use the median analyst earnings forecast made in the 30 days prior to the earnings announcement as our proxy for what market expectations were. Earnings-surprise returns are measured over either a 3-day window or a 21-day window surrounding the earnings announcement date. Importantly, all announcement returns are adjusted for the (value-weight) market returns over the same period, so we can isolate the performance of the specific company without thinking about general market movements. These are called *excess* or *market-adjusted* returns. Last, we focus on annual earnings surprises because there are more forecasts for annual earnings than for quarterly earnings. We should note that all these details are fairly standard and well-accepted ways of measuring our variables, but none of the results we discuss are dependent on them. The results are incredibly robust to alternative ways of measuring these variables.

After we measure all our variables, we place each of the earnings surprises in one of three groups: positive surprises (where reported earnings are greater than expectations), zero surprises (where reported earnings equal expectations), and negative surprises (where reported earnings are less than expectations). In our sample, the positive surprises, zero surprises, and negative surprises account for 51%, 16%, and 33% of the total observations, respectively. Positive earnings surprises therefore account for about half of all surprises. And zero surprises (those that just meet expectations) are the least common type of announcement.

Figure 6.1 summarizes our findings for the 3-day window returns. The figure reports the distribution of earnings surprise returns for each of the three earnings surprise groups (specifically, the 90th, 75th, 50th, 25th, and 10th percentile of the distribution). Figure 6.1 contains several important messages. First, the median return was positive for positive surprises, close to zero for zero surprises, and negative for negative surprises. We can see this by examining the middle set of bars labeled Median, which represents the 50th percentile of returns for the three different earnings surprise groups. (Although it isn't shown in the figures, the *average* excess returns exhibited the same pattern: 1.44%, –0.27%, and –1.36% for the positive, zero, and negative surprise groups, respectively.) Thus, on average, positive earnings surprises were met with positive market reactions, zero earnings surprises were met with close-to-zero market reactions, and negative earnings surprises were met with negative market reactions. This makes sense. The second observation to make is that, as you scan to the left and right of the median reactions, at all points on the distribution, returns for positive earnings surprises were always higher than those for zero surprises. In turn, these were always higher than those for negative surprises. Again, this isn't too surprising.

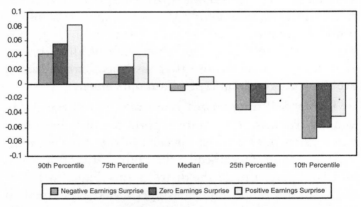

FIGURE 6.1   *Excess market reactions to earnings surprises over a 3-day window*

Market Reactions That Go in the Opposite Direction

Our third and most important observation is this: *Positive earnings surprises were not always good news, and negative earnings surprises were not always bad news.* We can see this by looking at essentially any of the sets of bars other than the middle median set. For example, consider the bars for the 25th percentile returns. First you'll note that negative earnings surprises at this 25th percentile mark had fairly negative returns, coming in at about –4%. But the main point is that even the positive earnings surprises had a *negative* market reaction; here, they're clocked at about –2%. Let's repeat that. *Positive* earnings surprises were being met with *negative* market reactions on the order of –2% when we look at the 25th percentile returns. Examining the 10th percentile returns (the set of bars on the far right), the news is even worse, with positive earnings surprises clocking about a –5% return. And these are all excess returns, above and beyond that of the market in general.

When we move to the other side of the distribution, the message is essentially the same. For instance, consider the 90th percentile returns (the set of bars on the far left). Again, positive earnings surprises here were met with positive returns on the order of about 8%. But again, the news is in the negative earnings surprises. Here, these negative surprises were clocking 4% returns. Indeed, even the announcements where companies are just meeting expectations (the zero earnings surprise group) were being met with close to 6% market reactions.

Figure 6.2 summarizes similar findings for the 21-day window. Recall that the 21-day window starts 19 days before and one day after the earnings announcement. It is examined to allow for any information leakage that may occur due to earnings preannouncements and other forms of leakage. The overall results and conclusions are identical to those of the shorter 3-day window. Note that the two figures look very similar, but the scale on the y-axis is –10% to 10% for the 3-day return and –20% to 20% for the 21-day window. Thus, the magnitude of market reactions to earnings surprises is much larger over the 21-day window than over the 3-day window. Overall, positive earnings surprises were rewarded by the market, and negative earnings surprises were punished. The mean excess returns over the 21-day period for positive, zero, and negative earnings surprises were 2.38%, 0.09%, and –2.50%, respectively. However, even over this much longer period, positive surprises were not always good news and negative surprises were not always bad news. The 25th percentile returns for positive earnings surprises were negative, and the 75th percentile returns for negative earnings surprises were positive. We draw similar conclusions from the 10th and 90th percentiles.

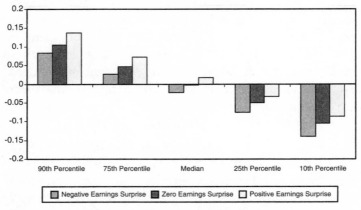

FIGURE 6.2   *Excess market reactions to earnings surprises over a 21-day window*

The most surprising finding in these figures is that an overwhelming number of positive earnings surprises were met with negative market reactions, and vice versa for the negative earnings surprises. However, we haven't yet tabulated the precise occurrence of these *opposite reaction* events. Table 6.1 provides the counts in our sample.

TABLE 6.1 *Proportion of Positive and Negative Excess Returns for Positive, Zero, and Negative Earnings Surprises*

	3-Day Window Return		21-Day Window Return	
	Positive (≥0)	Negative (<0)	Positive (≥0)	Negative (<0)
Positive surprises	60.55%	39.45%	59.18%	40.82%
Zero surprises	48.46%	51.54%	48.39%	51.61%
Negative surprises	38.95%	61.05%	37.49%	62.51%

The numbers in Table 6.1 clearly show that it is very common for earnings surprises to have returns of the opposite sign. For example, over the 3-day window, 39.45% of the positive earnings surprises had negative returns, and 38.95% of the negative earnings surprises had positive returns. Over the 21-day window, 40.82% of the positive earnings surprises had negative announcement returns, and 37.49% of the negative surprises had positive announcement returns. This finding is important because it implies that, even if you are very good at forecasting earnings surprises, you can still incur significant trading losses, because the market reactions so often go in the opposite direction.

A study by Kinney, Burgstahler, and Martin (2002) reached similar conclusions using a different sample and different research design. The authors collected over 22,000 actual annual earnings and forecasts from 1992 to 1997.[1] Not surprisingly, the authors found that, on average, positive surprises were good news and negative surprises were bad news. However, within all their earnings-surprise-ranked portfolios, no matter how large the positive or negative surprises were, many companies' earnings announcement returns have the opposite sign of the earnings surprise. Of all the positive surprise portfolios, the maximum proportion of companies with positive returns was 62%, far less than the 100% that many people may have suspected. Of all the negative surprise portfolios, the maximum proportion of companies with negative returns was only 58%. Thus, even with perfect hindsight into the direction of earnings surprises, an investor would lose money at least 38% of the time for positive surprises and 42% of the time for negative ones. Moreover, the authors found that the market reacted more strongly as the magnitude of earnings surprises increased. However, the market's reaction to earnings surprises tended to flatten when earnings surprises became increasingly larger. When the magnitude of an earnings surprise was already very large, increasing the magnitude further had little effect on the market's reaction. For instance, a company's stock price may go up much more with a $0.10 positive surprise relative to a $0.05 surprise, but a $2.00 surprise may not get much more action than a $1.50 surprise.

Why do so many earnings surprises have returns of the opposite sign? There are (at least) two explanations for this phenomenon. First, the earnings surprises we calculate are not the "true" earnings surprises. As we discussed in Chapter 3, "Earnings Surprises: Definition and Measurement," neither actual earnings nor earnings expectations are directly observable. If the proxies we use are imperfect, which they certainly are, the earnings surprises we calculate can deviate from the "true" earnings surprises. This means that some of the earnings surprises that we (and the *Wall Street Journal*, the *Financial Times*, and so on) deem positive may actually be negative. We simply don't have the technology or know-how to precisely measure the magnitude and direction of the earnings surprise. The second explanation is related to our discussion in Chapter 2, "Earnings Announcements: Why Are They So Important?" about the actual content of an earnings announcement: Managers of companies tend to release other information besides just the actual earnings number. So other good news could be released when negative earnings surprises are announced (such as new information about cost-cutting initiatives), or other bad news could be released when positive surprises are announced (such as dire forecasts for future earnings). If the other news contained in the announcement outweighs or dominates the earnings surprise, the net effect can be a market reaction that has the opposite sign of the earnings surprise. The story of Research in Motion (NASDAQ: RIMM) in Chapter 1, "Introduction," is a perfect example. RIMM announced a positive earnings surprise, but its revenue outlook was weaker than analysts expected. The market seemed to weigh the future revenue outlook more than the present positive earnings surprise, which ultimately resulted in a large negative price reaction to the positive earnings surprise.

Whatever the reason, the finding that many earnings surprises are associated with returns of the opposite sign suggests that it can be very risky to make directional (bullish, bearish) bets on earnings surprises.

Empirical Evidence Across Time

We've documented the *opposite reaction* phenomenon across different levels of earnings surprises. Next, let's take a look at time-series evidence by examining how the earnings-surprise return distributions have changed over time, in each year from 1984 to 2009. As we did in the preceding chapter, the purpose of this test is to examine whether the market's reactions to earnings surprises have become less significant over the years.

Figure 6.3 is for the 3-day window return. To avoid overcrowding the graph, we plot only the 25th and 75th percentile returns. Figure 6.3 shows that the patterns we observe for the sample as a whole also existed in each of the 26 years of our sample. Specifically, the 75th percentile returns were always positive and the 25th percentile returns were always negative, regardless of the sign of the earnings surprise. For instance, even for the negative earnings surprises, the 75th percentile returns for these negative surprises were always met by positive market reactions. Our analysis shows that 2006 was the year in which negative earnings surprises were the closest to being negative, but even in this year, the 75th percentile returns earned close to 1%. In the years since then, returns have actually *increased* for these negative surprises. There's similar evidence for the positive earnings surprises. Here, consider the 25th percentile returns for the positive earnings surprises. They were always negative, with the years 2000 and 2009 representing the most anomalous years, where the positive surprises were met with over a −3% market-adjusted reaction.

Overall, no evidence exists that this *opposite reaction* phenomenon is diminishing over the years. And even when we do not consider the opposite reactions and simply consider market reactions in general, evidence exists that the market reactions seem to be trending upward over time. In the last 2 years (2008 and 2009), the 75th percentile returns were much higher and the 25th percentile returns were much lower than they were in prior years. Certainly the spike in market volatility due to recent events such as the financial crisis are contributing to this finding.

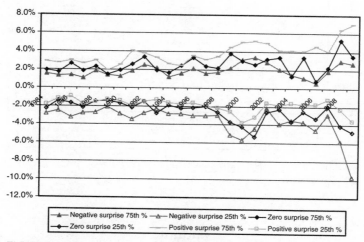

FIGURE 6.3 *Excess market reactions to earnings surprises over a 3-day window*

Last, Figure 6.4 presents similar evidence when we consider a longer, 21-day window. As before, extending the window for which we cumulate returns only seems to exaggerate our findings over the 3-day window.

Now, instead of talking about returns in the 2% to 6% range, the market returns are in the 5% to 10% range. As before, opposite reactions are commonplace and do not seem to be dying over time. Again, a case can be made that market reactions overall are becoming *more* severe, not less.

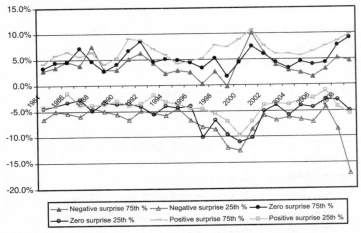

FIGURE 6.4 *Excess market reactions to earnings surprises over a 21-day window*

Endnote

1. *The authors measured earnings surprises as actual earnings minus the last consensus forecast divided by the stock price. They ranked the earnings surprises and formed several portfolios of 500 earnings-surprise observations each. Returns associated with earnings announcements were measured as the 22-day market-adjusted returns.*

Part IV

Implementation: Options Trading Strategies

Part III presented evidence of how the market reacts to earnings announcements and earnings surprises. We discussed how large these market reactions are compared to typical trading days, and we also showed how a surprisingly large portion of these market reactions are in the *opposite direction* of the earnings surprise. Part IV discusses several different ways to extract gains from options-based trading strategies that exploit these empirical regularities. Our goal is to tailor these strategies to fit into your arsenal of how to exploit these short-term trading windows targeted around companies' earnings announcements.

Chapter 7 describes the unique characteristics of companies that have listed options, as well as the behavior of these options around earnings announcement days. **Chapter 8** discusses many of the practical considerations you need to consider before implementing a trade. **Chapter 9** presents examples of directional options trades, including long calls and puts, as well as bull call spreads and bear put spreads. **Chapter 10**—our main trading chapter that exploits the uncertainty behind opposite-direction market reactions—presents examples of long straddle and strangle trades, as well as short iron butterflies and short iron condors. **Chapter 11** considers short straddles and strangles.

Chapter 7

General Characteristics of Optioned Companies and Options Behavior Around Earnings Announcements

Before we begin our discussion of specific types of option trades, we should discuss the proverbial forest versus the trees. We'll concentrate on describing some of the general phenomena around options trading, as well as some of the general characteristics of companies that have options listed on the Chicago Board Options Exchange (CBOE) (versus those that don't). This discussion provides a strong economic and intuitive background for and understanding of the environment within which you're trading but are taking for granted.

The Nature of Companies That Have Listed Options (Versus Those That Don't)

Not all publicly traded companies have options listed for trading. Obviously, in our options-trading strategies we care about companies that have options available to trade. This is by definition. So, if we can't trade companies without options, what's the point of making a distinction between the two? We believe it's still important for the options trader to be aware of the salient differences between optioned companies and nonoptioned companies. This will help you understand some of the more subtle implications of trading in optioned companies. For stock-based traders who are thinking about taking the plunge into options trading, this discussion is particularly useful, because it lays out some of the key distinctions you should be aware of.

First, we've known for many years that optioned companies tend to be larger, more liquid companies. In a study by Ho (1993), the author examined the full universe of all publicly traded companies and found that optioned companies, when compared with nonoptioned companies, were larger in market capitalization, higher in institutional ownership, higher in analyst coverage, and higher in trading volume. Optioned companies also tended to have more news articles published about them. These characteristics imply that optioned companies are operating in a world where the amount of public information about the company that is circulating out there is far, deep, and wide when compared to smaller, more obscure companies that do not have listed options. Because an army of financial analysts are helping get even the smallest bits of information into the market, and thousands of sophisticated institutional investors are exploiting such information, even *private* information about the company will be better reflected in its underlying equity price.[1]

Earnings Announcements and Optioned Versus Nonoptioned Companies

A study by Roll, Schwartz, and Subrahmanyam (2009) found that options trading around earnings announcements has been steadily increasing every year since 1996. Before we begin with specific trading strategies, it makes sense to get a sense of the general behavior of options around earnings announcement periods.

The idea that companies with listed options have a larger amount of information impounded into their stock prices makes intuitive sense. And this is precisely what a study by Amin and Lee (1997) found about optioned companies. They found that this *better infor-mation impounding* happened for optioned companies in both their earnings announcement periods and their non-earnings-announcement periods—basically, all the time. Another study by Jennings and Starks (1986) uncovered evidence that's consistent with this. They found that the price adjustment to earnings news (in the immediate aftermath of an announcement) is faster for optioned companies than it is for nonoptioned companies. What this discussion means for you in a practical sense is that it is unlikely that you, as an individual investor with limited resources, will have a consistent informational advantage over the market as a whole or over more sophisticated institutional investors. This has some major implications for your options-based trading strategies, which we'll discuss later. (Namely, you'll be unable to consistently discover true *mispricings*.)

Several studies have considered this issue with respect to options prices. Specifically, Ho (1993) found that, for optioned companies, 50% of earnings-related information is reflected in a company's stock price even before the earnings announcement is made. Part of this is certainly because earnings information probably is leaked early. However, even if there were no information leak, this suggests that sophisticated institutional investors are estimating earnings accurately before they are announced. Contrast that with companies that have no options listed or traded. Remember, nonoptioned companies tend to be small-cap companies that not as many people pay attention to. Ho found that for nonoptioned companies, only about 30% of the information is reflected in prices before the earnings announcement. This large difference (50% versus 30%) indicates that it is much harder to gain an information advantage for optioned companies. Indeed, several studies examine this issue. For instance, a study by Mendenhall and Fehrs (1999) and another by Kim and Lee (2006) suggest that, if you are an *informed trader* with valuable information that the public does not have... Well, where would *you* go to extract the biggest bang for your buck? That's right: You'd go to the options markets.[2] So these studies found that the market reaction to earnings information is *bigger* in optioned companies because it is full of informed traders who put on leveraged positions to best exploit their information. Many investment websites and blogs take the time to tell their readers about large options positions that have recently been opened for certain companies. The idea is that if an investor has the money to put on such a large options position, chances are that he or she knows something we don't know.

Behavior of Options Prices Before and During the Earnings Announcement

Let's move on to talk about the period before earnings are announced—the preannouncement period. In the preannouncement period, we know that smart money puts on trades to exploit their superior information. Amin and Lee's 1997 study confirms this. They found that more long call positions and short put positions were opened before positive earnings surprises. Similarly, they found that more long put and short call trades were put on before bad earnings surprises. Although we can't know for sure whether these directional option positions were profitable (because of what we know about the opposite reactions we discussed in Chapter 6, "Market Reactions to Earnings Surprises (Are Full of Surprises)," <u>it's clear that the options positions</u> seem to be <u>anticipating the nature of the earnings news</u> before the news is <u>announced.</u> This is consistent with Ho's 1993 finding that a fairly large portion—up to 50%—of information can be impounded into prices in the period right before earnings are announced. Roll, Schwartz, and Subrahmanyam (2009) also found that this effect was even stronger for companies that had a relatively higher number of analysts who follow the company and for companies with higher levels of institutional ownership. As usual, it's the presence of these big players that makes it relatively more difficult to put on profitable trades—at least directional trades that are either bullish or bearish.

For more than 30 years, when a study by Patell and Wolfson (1979) was published, we have also known that the implied volatility of options tends to increase in the earnings preannouncement period. This is because nerves are frayed in the frenzied anticipation of the news. On average, implied volatilities tend to be higher than realized/historical volatilities. But the difference is even more pronounced right before earnings announcements. A study by Donders, Kouwenberg, and Vorst (2000) found similar increases in the open interest and trading volume of options in the preannouncement period. And the higher the options trading volume in the preannouncement period, the stronger the *price anticipation* during this period. (A study by Corrado and Truong (2009) also confirms this.) In general, these studies suggest that much action occurs in the preannouncement period. This isn't surprising. Earnings announcements are the most prominent, regularly recurring corporate event for publicly traded companies.

Last, how things happen in the preannouncement period can predict how things will play out during the actual earnings announcement. Another finding of the Roll, Schwartz, and Subrahmanyam (2009) study is that higher trading volume in the preannouncement period tends to equate to less trading volume for the market reaction to the announcement itself. This makes sense. The more the action has been impounded into option prices in the preannouncement period, the less action the actual announcement will have. After all, only so much news can get impounded. The authors also found that, if relative options trading volume is high when the announcement happens (such as during the announcement day), the change in option prices also tends to be higher. That is, higher volume is related to bigger price action (regardless of the preannouncement trading volume).

Endnotes

1. *The general richness or opaqueness of a company's information set is discussed further in Chapter 15, "Other Theories and Evidence."*

2. *The idea that informed traders may try to exploit their informational advantage by trading in options instead of the underlying equity makes one naturally ask whether stocks or options lead. That is, do option prices give you a peek into the future movement of stock prices? Or is it the other way around? A number of studies in recent years (including Easley et al., 1998; Chakravarty et al., 2004; and Chan et al., 2002) found that options order flows tended to lead stock order flows. This suggests that looking at changes in bid/ask spreads or quotes of options can give you insight into imminent, upcoming movements in the underlying equity prices. Pan and Poteshman (2006) found that the ratio of puts to calls on newly opened positions can predict the movement of stock prices up to one week in advance. And this predictive power was even stronger for relatively smaller firms.*

Chapter 8

Practical Considerations Before Implementing Trades

Before we start discussing the various types of options trades you can enter or open, we need to discuss some of the practical issues you must consider first. We discussed much of the philosophy behind our keep-it-simple approach to options trading in the Preface. Overly complex options trades (or even overly complex *analysis*) do not necessarily earn you higher returns. However, you still need to consider some fundamental aspects of the trades. This chapter discusses these aspects.

Earnings Announcement Calendar

To trade around earnings announcements, first you must have an idea of when earnings announcements for companies are scheduled to take place. Several sources are available for obtaining this information. The most popular one is the *Wall Street Journal*'s earnings calendar, which can be found at http://online.wsj.com/mdc/public/page/markets_calendar.html. (The *Wall Street Journal* gets its earnings announcement dates from Thomson Reuters, the major source of earnings-related data.) On this earnings calendar page, you can find the dates of *earnings releases* (essentially the earnings announcement date), as well as the date of a company's conference call. These dates are separated into those that are confirmed and those that are estimated. Confirmed dates have been confirmed with the company. Estimated dates have not been confirmed per se, but given prior information about each company's earnings announcement history, the *Wall Street Journal* has made an estimate. In any case, you can click any of the dates (by day or week) on the calendar, scrolling forward to whatever future month you like. (You can also scroll back to get a sense of prior months' announcements.) Last, if you're looking for a particular company's expected earnings announcement date, you can search for it using either the company name or its ticker symbol.

Ready to Make a Prediction About the Market Reaction?

After you've determined the company and the earnings announcement date, you might (repeat: *might*) have to make a professional judgment about what you expect the earnings announcement will be like. Will the company announce a positive or negative earnings surprise? Given the evidence we talked about in Chapter 6, "Market Reactions to Earnings Surprises (Are Full of Surprises)," you must then also make a *separate* assessment of what you believe the market reaction to the earnings surprise will be. As we've stressed before, the earnings surprise and the market reaction need not go in the same direction. Indeed, about 40% of the time, they go in opposite directions. In the end, your prediction of this ultimate market reaction (not the underlying earnings surprise) will be the main factor that determines the type of options position that will be opened.

Your prediction of the market reaction will be based on many factors. It depends on your assessment of the company's performance over the previous fiscal quarter, and how that performance will be reflected in the upcoming earnings announcement. It also depends on how that earnings performance ultimately compares to consensus or market expectations. As we discussed in Chapters 3 and 4, these are not easy, cut-and-dried issues. Remember, plenty of smart financial analysts working for large investment houses, with the backing of huge resources (technology and staff), use sophisticated models and still cannot accurately predict earnings. It's a tough game. It takes rigorous fundamental analysis (material that is beyond the scope of this book). Even if you predict the earnings surprise accurately, your prediction of the ultimate market reaction will further depend on any other information that the company may divulge during the earnings announcement, including its forecast of future quarters' performance. Management's forecast—as well as your own—will be driven by an objective assessment of the general conditions in which the company operates, the industry in which it operates, and the overall economy. Importantly, the overall sentiment of the market at the time of the announcement can also have an effect.[1] In the end, many factors go into the ultimate market reaction. If you knew the perfect answer to this age-old question, you would be rich. Chapters 4 and 6 discussed some of the issues involved in predicting these market reactions. To the extent that you've done your homework and have confident predictions about the market reaction around earnings surprises, you'll be opening bullish or bearish positions according to your predictions. In the coming chapters, we devote much space to what we believe are the best option trades when it's too difficult to predict these market reactions.

Choosing the Right Strike Price

Open contracts that are very close to at-the-money. If you can't, due to an uneven stock price, enter into the closest in-the-money or out-of-the-money contract you can. Choosing strike prices that are further out-of-the-money or very in-the-money each has its pros and cons. We do not discuss these issues in detail here, because they have been covered by many other books. The main point is that an option's delta is near 1 for at-the-money options. This is where we get a very high level of response in the option price compared to the movements in the underlying equity. Ultimately, the choice of strike price is a balance between having a high delta position without having to pay too high a price. In-the-money options cost more than out-of-the-money options. In terms of percentage returns, choosing out-of-the-money options can be more profitable than in-the-money options if the underlying stock price movement upon earnings announcement is large enough to approach the out-of-the-money strike. However, the *probability* of earning these higher returns is lower.

Choosing the Right Expiration Month

Choose option contracts in the closest/nearest expiration month, because they have the highest delta. This is particularly important, because all the strategies we discuss in this book are *short-term* strategies. They begin a few days before earnings announcements and end a day or two afterward. However, if the date of the earnings announcement is close to the options expiration date, open your trade in the following month's contract. When the contract is too close to expiration, the issue of time decay becomes even more significant than usual and can eat up a lot of the option's value. This will ultimately dampen the large price movements you are hoping for. (For a short-option position, you want exactly this type of time decay; we talk about this in Chapter 11, "Short Straddle and Strangle Strategies.") Choosing a further-out expiration month also gives you the flexibility to continue your trade after the earnings announcement, if you deem this the proper strategy. Regardless, for purposes of trading around earnings announcement dates, never choose contracts that are too far out, because they simply do not respond as sensitively to earnings news. They also tend to be much less liquid, which translates into higher trading costs. We talk about this issue more next.

The Role of Trading Volume

The level of trading volume that exists for an options contract can have a significant impact on not only the profitability of your trades, but even the *probability* that a trade can get executed at all. Before talking about the specifics, let's spend a few minutes talking about the theory.

In a study by Landsman and Maydew (2002), the authors showed that trading volume (as well as volatility) of equity securities tended to spike during earnings announcement periods. This volume spike has been increasing in recent years. (Similar evidence was documented over 30 years before by Beaver (1968).) From a general point of view, this is good news, because it further corroborates our thesis that earnings announcements are excellent events to trade on. For the trading volume of options contracts in particular, Corrado and Truong (2009) found a huge amount of variation in the amount of trading volume in options contracts. Specifically, they found that, during a typical 3-day earnings announcement period, a full 37% of the universe of listed options had fewer than 100 contracts that were traded; that averages to about 33 contracts a day. That's pretty thinly traded. Indeed, plenty of contracts don't trade at all for several days or even weeks—and this is for large-cap stocks such as Microsoft. This typically happens with very out-of-the-money, back-month (far-dated) expiration contracts. In the same study, the authors found that only 19% of options had more than 2,000 contracts traded during the earnings announcement period. These options contracts have the highest levels of liquidity that allow less-frictioned trading to take place. Corrado and Truong (2009) also found that trading volume was a very good proxy for whether informed traders could *act* on their private/superior information. Therefore, the options markets can play a prominent role in *price discovery* (where new information is embedded into prices to help discover a new intrinsic value), but *only* when options volumes are high enough. (Similar conclusions are made by Chakravarty,

Gulen, and Mayhew (2004).) Another study by Pan and Poteshman (2006) found that the ratio of puts to calls on newly opened positions predicted the movement of stock prices up to a week in advance. And this predictive power was even stronger for relatively smaller companies. In general, the evidence suggests that options prices seem to reflect *new* news in a quicker, more efficient manner than the underlying equity stock prices, but the conditions have to be right.[2] For instance, Admati and Pfleiderer (1988) found that in thinly traded options markets, informed traders couldn't sufficiently exploit their superior information. The bid-ask spreads were so large that they overwhelmed any informational advantage that such traders had.

Overall, the evidence suggests that thinly traded markets are relatively more dangerous to trade in. From a practical standpoint, you should therefore be particularly cautious when entering orders in contracts that have fewer than 50 contracts traded on an average day. There are always exceptions to rules of thumb, so use the fewer-than-50 rule judiciously. But such thinly traded markets can rarely be the place of consistently profitable trades, especially when implementing short-term trades. We've already discussed our philosophy of efficient pricing in options markets. Briefly, we believe that most options contracts are fairly efficiently priced. Even when they're mispriced, individual investors are outgunned by the big boys anyway, making our ability to *consistently* exploit mispricings quite small. From a practical point of view, this is great news, because it enables you to examine trading opportunities without the burden of having to seek out small mispricings. After all, if everything is efficiently priced, you need only look for good trading opportunities based on predictions of the news reactions of the underlying equity. The one important caveat of our efficient-pricing philosophy occurs when dealing in options contracts that are thinly traded. In such markets, mispricings can be rampant and commonplace. This is mostly because of the large spreads between the bid and ask prices (which we discuss next). On the other hand, deeply traded options contracts have trading volume in the thousands. In such markets, there is little to fear about significant mispricings.

For a typical example of trading volumes along options chains, consider Advanced Micro Devices (NYSE: AMD). Its closing price on August 19, 2010 was $6.42. Consider the September expiration contract (because the August contract essentially has one more trading day before expiration). Look at the trading volume for the nearest in-the-money call option, the $6 strike. Trading volume for the day was 173 contracts. As far as options contracts go, this is a fair amount of volume. The $7 strike had a trading volume of 740 contracts. This is a fairly deep market. For the $9 strike, trading volume for the day was 0. As a percentage of price, bid-ask spreads typically are larger as the trading volume gets thinner. We discuss this issue of bid-ask spreads next.

Bid-Ask Spreads

The notion of trading volume is intimately related to that of bid-ask spreads. Bid-ask spreads represent the difference between what one side is willing to buy at (the bid) versus what the other side is willing to sell at (the ask). For instance, for the AMD September 6 call, the bid is $0.61 and the ask is $0.63. The difference of

$0.02 is the bid-ask spread. As a percentage of the average (of the bid and ask) price, the spread is 3.2% of the price. This isn't bad.

Although trading volume is an important metric, in the end it's not trading volume that affects your profitability, but the bid-ask spread. The point is that the bid-ask spread and trading volume are highly (inversely) correlated: Bid-ask spreads tend to be low when trading volume is high, and vice versa. But nonetheless, it's the bid-ask spread that determines your entry and exit prices, not trading volume per se. In thinly traded options markets—particularly common in contracts that are far-dated or very out-of-the-money—the bid-ask spread can be extremely large, making the probability of a profitable trade all the more difficult. This is particularly true in short-term trades where you must fight against the spread in both directions—once when you're opening the trade, and again when you're closing it. Admati and Pfleiderer (1988) found that in thinly traded options markets, informed traders could not sufficiently exploit their superior information because the bid-ask spread became so large.

Most of the examples in this book are of large-cap companies, with option contracts that were deliberately chosen as near-month expiration and at-the-money (or very close in- or out-of-the-money). Such option contracts typically are the most liquid of those listed on the CBOE. This means that bid-ask spreads are fairly narrow. For instance, on August 13, 2010, Bank of America (NYSE: BAC) closed at $13.23. Its August 13 call options have a bid of $0.37 and an ask of $0.39, a spread of $0.02. Although it represents about 5.3% of the price, this spread is fairly normal. (Whether you view the spread as high or low is a matter of opinion.) The August 14 call has a bid of $0.04 and an ask of $0.05. The $0.01 spread is currently the best that you'll get, but note that it represents a huge percentage of the contract price. Regardless, the point is that the spreads are fairly manageable in this scenario.

However, as we move into smaller-cap companies, options trading volume can become quite low. This increases our chances that we're trading in an option that doesn't have all its value-relevant information impounded into its price. However, the larger bid-ask spreads will add a fairly high cost to our trading strategy. For instance, consider China Natural Gas (NASD: CHNG), a small-cap Chinese energy company. On August 13, 2010, CHNG closed at $6.64. Its August 5 strike call, which is in-the-money, has a bid of $1.50 and an ask of $1.75. The bid-ask spread here is $0.25. This represents about 15% of the price. Similarly, the August $7.50 put, which is also in-the-money, has a bid of $0.80 and an ask of $1.05—again a $0.25 spread, this time representing about 27% of the price. These are *huge* spreads, and they make it very difficult to be consistently profitable in short-term trades. The problem is twofold. First, opening such a position means getting in at the worst price. So if you were opening a long position, you would have to buy at the asking price. The second problem is that you must then exit the trade at the worst price as well. So if you exit the trade a few days later, you would have to sell at the bidding price. This means that, for your trade to be profitable, a huge swing in the underlying equity must occur that translates into very large movements in the option price to compensate for the bad entry and exit points arising from the wide spreads. Opening a *straddle* position (discussed in Chapters 10 and 11) only doubles the pain, because you must enter into two separate option contracts (both the puts and the calls). Beware the bid-ask spread.

In practice, sometimes it is possible to enter your trade as a limit order at somewhere near the midpoint of the bid and ask. For instance, in the case of Bank of America's bid of $0.37 and ask of $0.39, you could enter a limit order of $0.38, just to test the waters. The trade may get executed immediately at your limit price. Or the order may linger in the queue for a few minutes and then get executed. Or the order may not get executed at all. (In thinly traded markets, a midpoint limit order can wait in the queue for *hours* or *days* before an interested party decides to pick up your order.) The limit price you enter should obviously take into consideration these different possibilities. It is important to fight for every penny. But also be aware that sometimes you miss out on a profitable trade because you were "too cheap" to enter at the going ask price. Of course, the opposite also happens. You may miss a trade because of your cheapness and then find that the trade would have turned against you anyway. In that case, you're quite glad that your limit order didn't get executed.

Choose a fairly aggressive limit-order price—perhaps one tick away from the bid price. Then, if the order doesn't execute, simply change your order to a price that is more acceptable by the other side. This tactic has a couple advantages. First, especially for fairly illiquid option contracts, sometimes the bids and asks are fairly stale to begin with, representing orders from hours—even days—earlier. (See Easley, O'Hara, and Srinivas (1998) and Chakravarty, Gulen, and Mayhew (2004) for studies that have examined this stale pricing issue.) If this is the case, you may sometimes enter an order that gets executed immediately because the underlying equity price has moved in such a way that the limit price you entered is greedily gobbled up by someone at the least favorable price to you. Second, when putting in an aggressive price, if it does not execute, changing the order does not incur any additional transaction costs. However, one downside of this strategy is that, in fast-moving markets, you may find that your order is simply too late to get filled, because the underlying equity quickly moves away from you. In these cases, with perfect hindsight, you may find that if you had simply entered a market order, you would have gotten it filled (at a fairly poor price for the moment), but the market then moved in your favor to more than make up for the poor price execution. Therefore, each approach has pros and cons that you should consider before executing a trade.

The last point worth mentioning concerns all-or-none orders. These orders are more difficult to fill when you pick aggressive limit-order prices. This is because the other side of the transaction must be willing to take your full order instead of a partial fill. Thus, an all-or-none order guarantees that you get the price you want for *all* your contracts, but it doesn't guarantee that the transaction will take place. On the other hand, a regular order increases the chances that your order will be at least partially filled at the price you entered. But you face the risk that you will not get all of your order filled, ultimately incurring full transaction costs for a fraction of the desired contracts.

Implied Volatility and Volatility Collapse

This section briefly discusses some of the core issues related to implied volatility. For a lengthier, more in-depth treatment of these issues, we recommend *The Volatility Edge in Options Trading*, an excellent book by Jeff Augen.

Option pricing theory, pioneered by Black and Scholes' (1973) classic study, tells us that an option's value is determined by several factors. These include the underlying stock's current price and volatility, the option's strike price and expiration date, and the current risk-free rate. Of all these factors, the stock's volatility is most subject to judgment and estimation. Suppose we were to calculate an option's theoretical price based on a stock price volatility that we calculate from a historical time-series of the stock's prices. This calculated price probably would be quite different from the price that the option is actually trading at. If we take the actual option price as a given, we can mathematically back into (or reverse-engineer) the volatility that is *implied* by the option price. This volatility is aptly called the option's *implied volatility*.

To evaluate whether an option is relatively cheap or expensive, compare the stock's *historical* volatility with its *implied* volatility (extracted from the option price). Implied volatilities typically are higher than historical volatilities. This has generally always been the case, even before option pricing theory was formally developed and even before options were officially listed on an exchange. (A study by Mixon (2009) examined option prices before the creation of the Black-Scholes model and before the CBOE was created.[3]) This is because option sellers ask for protection from very unusual, *black-swan*-type events. On average, although this difference in volatilities may be miniscule, it puts option buyers at a disadvantage, because this means that options are always overpriced relative to the theoretical prices dictated by historical volatility. Thus, when an option's implied volatility is very high compared to the stock's historical volatility, it is even harder for options buyers to squeeze profits out of a trade. On the other hand, when the implied volatility is relatively low, options buyers have a better chance to gain. (All this logic is reversed for options sellers.)

Implied volatilities often increase in the periods leading up to an earnings announcement (or any highly anticipated event, for that matter). This suggests that opening long options positions (which is essentially *buying volatility*) right before an earnings announcement is, all else equal, buying at a higher price. Alternatively, if a long position is built earlier, the buyer may reap additional profits from the increased implied volatility without even waiting for earnings to be announced. In fact, a compelling argument can be made against holding the straddle or strangle positions after earnings announcements. This is because *on average* the actual earnings announcement returns are less than what was implied by the option premiums. Another important nuance of volatility is that implied volatilities tend to diminish in the last hour of trading and tend to be higher in the opening hours of trading. This occurs because the market is digesting any developments that occurred during the 17.5 hours that it was closed. To the extent that this is true, it would be more profitable for an options buyer to close his position during the day rather than at the end of the day.

Just as implied volatility increases up to the point of an earnings announcement, it tends to drastically decrease in the period immediately following the announcement. This is called *volatility collapse*. This volatility collapse was documented at least 30 years ago in a study by Patell and Wolfson (1979). It is a phenomenon that is still alive and well today. The hope is that the movement in the underlying stock price more than compensates for this volatility collapse. To the extent that it doesn't, long option positions will be less profitable. These issues of volatility increases and decreases around earnings announcements can be particularly acute for positions that are at-the-money, because such volatility changes have a larger impact on the value of the positions. On the other hand, option positions that are very out-of-the-money are much less affected by changes in volatility because the probability of the stock price reaching such out-of-the-money strike prices is still fairly small.

Example 8.1: Volatility Collapse (NASDAQ: GOOG)

Google (NASDAQ: GOOG) is a major technology company with roughly $150 billion market capitalization; it's a powerhouse. In July 2010, with the ever-changing dynamic of the Internet ad business, it's no wonder that the market was closely watching and anticipating Google's upcoming earnings report. Anxiety about Google's performance—and the implications for the technology industry and the economy as a whole—was building to a crescendo.

After market close on July 15, 2010, Google announced earnings for its second fiscal quarter. It reported EPS of $6.450, missing the consensus forecast of $6.518 by $0.068, or 1.0%. As a result, Google's shares slumped from the previous close of $494.02 to a new close of $459.61, a decline of 7%. Options markets reacted similarly. The August 2010 490 calls collapsed from $22.18 to $5.10, close to close. The same strike/month puts increased from $18.50 to $34.80 over the same period. Although Google's stock price was punished, much of the anxiety, anticipation, and *uncertainty* about the results was resolved. This resolution of uncertainty is reflected in the pattern of its implied volatility.

Figure 8.1 shows the time series of implied volatility for Google's August 490 calls and puts options. Implied volatilities are presented for the 5 days before its earnings announcement—represented by the vertical dashed line—and the 5 days after. It is very clear that the July 15 announcement date was an inflection point for the implied volatilities. Implied volatilities for both options steadily increased from about 30% to 33%, a 10% increase. After the announcement, they sharply collapsed from 33% to about 23%, a 30% decrease.

Although the *level* of implied volatilities can reach much higher, this Google example illustrates the typical *evolution* of implied volatilities surrounding earnings announcements. Specifically, our empirical analysis suggests that the gradual increase in implied volatility in the days leading up to an earnings announcement typically is smaller than the volatility collapse that occurs immediately after such an announcement. This is not surprising. The market gradually builds up anxiety and anticipation in the days and weeks before an earnings announcement, and this is reflected in the rise in implied volatility. However, the earnings announcement is a clear event that occurs. After it is announced, if uncertainty is resolved, it is resolved almost immediately and therefore triggers a volatility collapse.

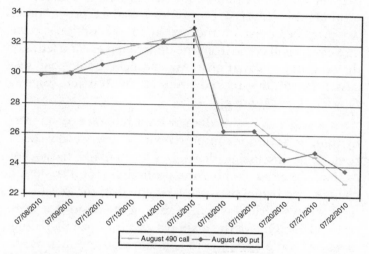

FIGURE 8.1   *Implied volatility for Google's (NASDAQ: GOOG) August 490 puts and August 490 calls for the 10 days surrounding the earnings announcement*

Entry and Exit Points

All the sample trades that we discuss in this book are short-term trades that last about 24 hours. In each example, we assume that you open the trade on the day before a company makes its earnings announcement, near market close for the day. We assume that you exit the trade the next day, again near market close, giving the market at least a few hours to digest the earnings announcement.

We do not discuss hourly, intraday fluctuations in option prices or the nuances of opening/closing the trades, say, 2 hours earlier or later from the closing times we've chosen. Discussing these types of decisions would detract from the pedagogical flow of our main thesis. It's not so much that the minute-by-minute fluctuations do not affect the profitability analysis of our trades. For the types of trades we propose, most of the action in the option's price movement will come from the underlying event itself, not the intraday fluctuations. An excellent book that discusses day-trading-related issues at length is Jeff Augen's *Day Trading Options*.

Although we don't discuss hour-by-hour or minute-by-minute deviations in entry/exit points, we do spend some time discussing deviations on a daily basis. For example, we discuss how the profitability of a trade can change (for better or worse) by entering the position a week or two earlier, as well as exiting the position a week or two later. One of the main reasons for opening a (long position) trade earlier is to capitalize on the increase in implied volatility that typically occurs in the days or weeks approaching a highly anticipated event such as a company's earnings announcement. On the other hand, the main argument against an early entry point is the significant time decay that occurs for front-month expiration option contracts. Deciding which of these opposing forces will ultimately dominate the option's pricing is an exercise we leave to you. We believe the detrimental effect of time decay is often underestimated and that the increase in implied volatility is often overestimated, suggesting that a later entry point is, on average, the most profitable decision. This is the main reason we suggest short-term trades that last a day or two.

As for extending the exit point of your trades, one of the main reasons for continuing to hold a position is to capitalize on any potential momentum that the stock price might experience in the days following the earnings release. A study by Pan and Poteshman (2006) found that profitable proprietary traders employed by investment houses tended to open options positions that take advantage of the momentum or drift in returns. Individual investors tended to do the opposite, opening options positions that traded against the momentum. Therefore, allowing the options position to exploit the short-term trend can be a profitable strategy. However, there are two sticking points. First, it's very difficult to predict whether a stock price's movement will continue with momentum or simply switch directions for a retracement/reversal. An attempt to reap further profits may simply wind up costing you the original profits as well. Second, because the options contracts are front-month contracts, time decay will become incredibly difficult to fight off if you are long options, because there are 10 days, 9 days, 8 days, and so on left till expiration. Thus, the hoped-for momentum must be strong enough to overpower the time decay. This time decay is a stronger force for the exit strategy than it is for the entry strategy simply because the proposed exit dates are closer to the contract's expiration date. For these reasons, we again suggest limiting the carry time on your trades to a 24-hour period.

Transaction Costs

We do not include transaction costs in any of our examples. These days, the competition among discount brokers has driven down transaction costs significantly. Typically they are in the range of $8 to $20 per trade (depending on the number of contracts traded). However, we do not want our silence about transaction costs to be interpreted to mean that they don't matter—they do. Transaction costs can eat into profits in a very big way. Be wary of how round-trip transaction costs are affecting your P&L. Depending on the number of trades you do, it's very possible that you'll accumulate literally thousands of dollars in transaction costs in a fiscal quarter.

Endnotes

1. *For a quirky study on how investor sentiment can affect these market reactions, see Shon and Zhou (2009).*

2. *Cao, Chen, and Griffin (2005) found that options volume predicted the future returns around corporate takeovers.*

3. *In a study by Mixon (2009), the author examined option prices of contracts that were traded in the 19th century, well before the introduction of the Chicago Board Options Exchange. He compared the option prices of the past to those of the current day. There have been incredible advances in the theory of option pricing over the past 50 years— most notably, the groundbreaking work of Black and Scholes (1973). Option pricing before 1973 was a fairly back-of-the-envelope practice that was not scientific or empiric priced, but done more by feel. Surprisingly, Mixon (2009) found that many of the empirical regularities that exist in today's option prices were essentially in existence even back then. Specifically, he found that the implied volatilities of 19th century options typically were higher than their historical/realized volatilities—as is the case today. He also found that implied volatilities were serially correlated in the 19th century, much like today. There was also significant comovement or correlation of implied volatilities among stocks back then, just as there is today. Last, there was skewness in implied volatility in the 19th century, as there is today. Overall, Mixon found that, even though there was no theory back then, option prices and how they behaved still resembled those of today. The empirical regularities we know of today are not driven solely by advances in theory. In fact, Mixon found that the driving factor that brought option prices closer to their theoretical (Black-Scholes) values was not the introduction of the theory itself, but the introduction of trading on the CBOE. Specifically, the gap between implied and historical volatilities really started disappearing (although not completely) after exchange trading of the options was introduced.*

Chapter 9

Directional Bets: Long Calls, Bull Call Spreads, Long Puts, and Bear Put Spreads

T his chapter begins our discussion of specific options trading strategies around earnings announcements. For the trades in this chapter, we assume that you've done your homework and have come up with directional predictions (bullish or bearish) for the market reactions to earnings surprises of particular companies you're interested in. We discuss the basic, directional options trades that you can put on, as well as some simple variations. But we caution you: Although these positions are simple to execute, we believe they are difficult to make consistent profits because of their simple, *directional* nature. You must correctly predict the direction (and magnitude) of the stock price—not an easy task.

Example 9.1: Long Call Position (NYSE: KFT)

This section describes a simple example of how to exploit a positive market reaction to a positive earnings surprise. This is a straightforward long position on a call option for Kraft Foods. A long call position assumes that you have a bullish view of Kraft. Compared to buying equity directly, a call option provides much higher potential upside in terms of rate of return if your bullish view is right. However, unlike buying equity with leverage, if your forecast is wrong, a call option limits your loss to your original investment, which is the premium you paid for the option position. In terms of risk-reward profile, the long call position uncaps reward potential and caps risk.

Kraft Foods (NYSE: KFT) is a multinational food company operating in over 70 countries. It manufactures and markets packaged food products such as snacks, beverages, and convenient meals. Warren Buffett is a long-term shareholder of Kraft because he believes in Kraft's long-term earnings power. On August 6, 2010, Kraft announced its earnings for its second fiscal quarter. On August 5, the day before its earnings announcement, Kraft's stock price closed at $29.66 (see Figure 9.1). At the time, the consensus analyst forecast for earnings was $0.52 per share. In the 2 weeks leading up to the earnings announcement, Kraft's price generally was trading between $29 and $30. If we are bullish on Kraft Foods and believe it will announce strong earnings that beat analysts' consensus forecast, we could express our view by implementing a long-call strategy. On the day before earnings were announced, we could have purchased the August expiration $30 strike price calls (which we can refer to as "August 30 calls") for $0.41. In the days leading up to the announcement, these calls were as low as $0.21. Here's an illustration of how option prices don't necessarily track the underlying equity prices on a one-to-one basis. Specifically, on the day before the announcement, on August 5, the $29.66 close on the stock price was· a decline from the day before, when it had closed at $29.75. However, the August 30 call closing at $0.41 represents an increase from the prior day's close of $0.35. This increase from $0.35 to $0.41 in the day before the earnings announcement cannot represent a tracking of the underlying stock price (because the stock price was down). Instead, it represents the increase in implied volatility that the call option reflected.

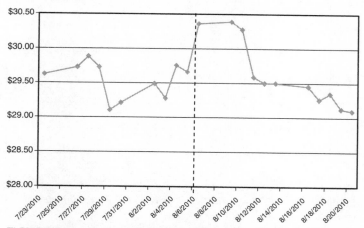

FIGURE 9.1 *Kraft Foods (NYSE: KFT) stock price in the 20 trading days surrounding the earnings announcement*

On August 6, Kraft announced earnings of $0.60 per share (see Figure 9.2), representing a 13% increase in earnings, and handily beating analysts' expectations. Kraft did, however, trim its expectation for near-term growth from 4% to a 3% to 4% range. Nonetheless, the stock price closed at $30.36, up 2.3%. This is an example of a positive earnings surprise met by a positive market reaction. Upon the earnings news and movement in the underlying stock price, the calls ended the next day at a price of $0.66, representing a 60.9% increase from our $0.41 purchase price. In dollar terms, if we had purchased 50 call contracts, the total purchase price would be $2,050. By the end of the day, our calls had increased in value to $3,300.

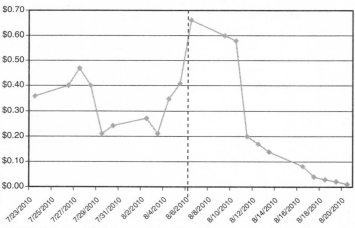

FIGURE 9.2   *KFT August 30 call price in the 20 trading days surrounding the earnings announcement*

Many types of momentum strategies would suggest that you continue holding onto your position after the good news. However, in this case, note that Kraft's stock price can retain its price increase for only about 3 more days before it starts to fall back to its pre-earnings announcement levels (as shown in Figure 9.1). Even in the immediate period after the earnings announcement, as Kraft's stock price inches upward again (closing on August 9 at $30.39), the call option's value (see Figure 9.2) cannot fight the decaying aspect of both the time decay over the weekend and the decline in implied volatility. Specifically, implied volatility declined from 22.68 on the day before the earnings announcement to 18.66 a day later, a 17.7% decline. Last, note the precipitous decline in the call's value as time decay dominates in the final days of the contract.

Table 9.1 summarizes the Kraft profits.

TABLE 9.1   *Profit from Long Call and Bull Call Spread Position (NYSE: KFT)*

	Stock Price	Long August 30 Call Price	Bull Call Spread Price, August 30 Call Plus August 31 Call
August 5, 2010	$29.66	$0.41	$0.30
August 6, 2010	$30.36	$0.66	$0.47
$ Change	$0.70	$0.25	$0.17
% Change	2.4%	60.9%	56.7%

Example 9.2: Bull Call Spread

You can implement several other types of option trades if you have a bullish view. We'll discuss a few of them here. The first, a bull call spread, is a position that is only moderately bullish. It is accomplished by first buying the call options, as we did in Example 9.1, and then also selling calls that are one (or more) strike price above the long call position. Essentially, you sell the calls to reduce the cost of your long position; that is the benefit. On the other hand, the disadvantage of this position is that any potential gain is muted. Last, be aware of the margin requirements for the short position.

For this example, we would initiate a bull call spread by first purchasing the August 30 calls for $0.41. And we would simultaneously sell, say, the August 31 calls, which were closing at $0.11. Because selling calls results in collecting a premium, this would reduce your total cost of the positions to $0.30 (= 0.41 − 0.11). So, if Kraft's stock price were to move downward the next day, although your August 30 long-call position would go down in value, so would the value of your August 31 short call. Thus, the short call subsidizes your long call. However, if Kraft's stock price were to move up the next day (as it did), although the August 30 long call would increase in value, so would the value of the August 31 short call. In this case, we know that the long August 30 call increases in value to $0.66. However, the short August 31 call also increases to $0.19. Thus, although we have a gain of $0.25 from the long call (= 0.66 − 0.41), we have a loss of $0.08 from the short call (= 0.11 − 0.19). This makes our total profit $0.17, which is calculated as the gain on the long call of $0.25 less the loss on the short call of $0.08. This bull call spread therefore has less downside risk but also has a capped upside due to the short call.

For the experienced trader who has studied the historical pattern of earnings announcement returns, a properly structured bull call spread can actually earn higher returns than a simple long call position. Specifically, you can choose a strike price for the short call leg of the spread that is sufficiently high enough (by historical standards) to ensure that it does not get reached. Such a strategy can be particularly useful when the earnings announcement date is very close to the option expiration date. This is because the value of the short out-of-the-money call will decrease sharply after the announcement due to both its volatility collapse and its exponentially-fast decay of time value. A more aggressive trader may consider implementing a ratio call strategy, which involves shorting more higher strike calls (for instance, at a 3:1 ratio), although the usual caveat of potentially unexpected large price movements applies here.

Last, note the severe collapse in the price of the August 31 call option in the days following the earnings announcement (see Figure 9.3).[1] Because the August 31 strike is further out-of-the-money, its collapse in price is inevitable (and very common) in the last few days of trading as the chance of an event that brings Kraft's stock price above $31 becomes all the more improbable. The skilled trader may have noticed this pattern and unwound the profitable leg of his bull call spread, the August 30 leg, and allowed the short August 31 leg to continue, because the decline is inevitable. However, leaving on a naked short call (because it is no longer hedged) has its own risks and should be done with caution.

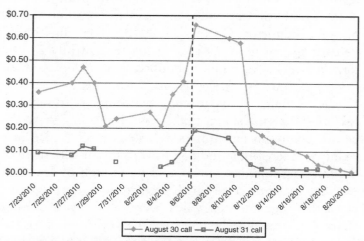

FIGURE 9.3   *KFT August 30 call and August 31 call prices in the 20 trading days surrounding the earnings announcement*

Example 9.3: Long Put Position (NYSE: EK)

Similar to the Kraft Foods example, now we discuss a simple example of how to exploit a negative market reaction to a negative earnings surprise. This is a straightforward long position on a put option for Eastman Kodak. A long put position assumes that you have a bearish view of Eastman Kodak. Compared to directly shorting the stock, a put option provides much higher potential upside in terms of rate of return if your bearish view is right. However, unlike shorting equity with leverage, if your forecast is wrong, a put option limits your loss to your original investment, which is the premium you paid for the option position. In terms of risk-reward profile, the long put position has uncapped reward potential (up to the point where the underlying equity goes to zero) and capped risk.

Eastman Kodak (NYSE: EK) sells imaging products, technology, solutions, and services, with products that span digital still and video cameras to consumer inkjet printers and media. On July 28, 2010, Kodak announced its earnings for its second fiscal quarter. On July 27, the day before its earnings announcement, Kodak's stock price closed at $4.93 (see Figure 9.4). At the time, consensus estimates were expecting the company to report a loss of –$0.28 per share. In the 2 weeks leading up to the earnings announcement, Kodak's stock price traded in a range between $4.30 and $5.06, with the July 27 price of $4.93 being one day after this 2-week high of $5.06. If we were to act on our bearish predictions, we would purchase the August 5 puts, which were selling for $0.39 per share. Like the underlying equity, the lowest point for the put was the previous day, trading at $0.34. It had been as high as $0.84 in the 2 weeks prior.

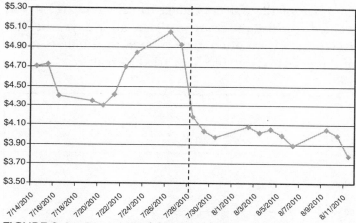

FIGURE 9.4 *Eastman Kodak (NYSE: EK) stock price in the 20 trading days surrounding the earnings announcement*

On July 28, Kodak announced that its accounting loss was –$0.51 per share (see Figure 9.5). This was a far cry from the expected –$0.28 per share. Kodak's stock price tanked, closing the day at $4.18, which represented a 15.2% decline. This is an example of a negative earnings surprise met by a negative market reaction. The $0.39 puts increased in value to close the day at $0.85. A purchase of 50 put contracts for $1,950 would have increased in value to $4,250 by the end of the next day, a 117.9% increase.

In this case, a momentum strategy would have worked quite well because the August 5 put stayed well within the money. The negative stock price reaction continued in the next few days as the market continued to digest the negative implications of the recent earnings announcement. However, capitalizing on this was difficult because of the lack of liquidity. The missing gaps in Figure 9.5 represent days of zero trading volume, where no buyers or sellers met an agreed-upon price. Although the price of the put continued to drift upward, if you wanted to close the trade in those latter days, the bid-ask spreads were often wide enough to eliminate much of the profit you would have tried to realize.

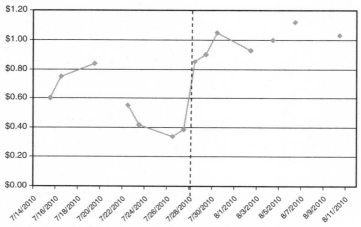

FIGURE 9.5 *EK August 5 put price in the 20 trading days surrounding the earnings announcement*

Table 9.2 summarizes the Kodak profits.

TABLE 9.2 *Profit from Long Put and Bear Put Spread Position (NYSE: EK)*

	Stock Price	Long August 5 Put Price	Bear Put Spread Price, August 5 Put Plus August 4 Put
July 27, 2010	$4.93	$0.39	$0.29
July 28, 2010	$4.18	$0.85	$0.70
$ Change	–$0.75	$0.46	$0.41
% Change	–15.2%	117.9%	141.3%

Example 9.4: Bear Put Spread

Much like the bull call spread, we could implement a similar spread for the bearish put position. It is called a bear put spread and is moderately bearish. It is accomplished by first buying the put options as we did in the previous example and then also selling puts that are one (or more) strike price below the long put position. Much like the bull call spread in Example 9.2, you sell the puts to reduce the cost of your long position, at the price of muting your potential gains.

For the Kodak example, we would initiate a bear put spread by first purchasing the August 5 puts for $0.39 (see Figure 9.6). And we would simultaneously sell the August 4 puts, which were closing at $0.10. Because selling puts results in collecting a premium, this would reduce your total cost of the positions to $0.29 (= 0.39 − 0.10). If Kodak's stock price were to move upward the next day, although your long August 5 puts would go down in value, so would the value of your short August 4 puts. Thus, the short put subsidizes your long put. However, if Kodak's stock price were to move downward the next day (as it did), although the long August 5 puts would increase in value, so would the value of the short ones. In this case, we know that the long put increases in value to $0.85. However, the short put also increases to $0.15. Thus, although we have a gain of $0.46 from the long put (= 0.85 − 0.39), we have a loss of $0.05 from the short put (= 0.15 − 0.19). This loss may be relatively small in absolute terms compared to the movement in the long put, but it still represents a 26.3% movement in its price. Overall, this makes our total profit $0.41, which is calculated as the gain on the long put of $0.46 less the

loss on the short put of $0.05. This bear put spread there-
fore has less downside risk. In this case, it actually has a
higher upside return (although the upside is ultimately
capped due to the short put). This is largely due to the
August 4 put remaining out-of-the-money even with this
large downside move. The August 4 put's delta is much
lower compared to the August 5 put's delta (which is near
1). Therefore, it requires very large moves in the underlying equity (in this case, larger than the 15.2% decline that
Kodak actually experienced) to experience large moves in
absolute terms.

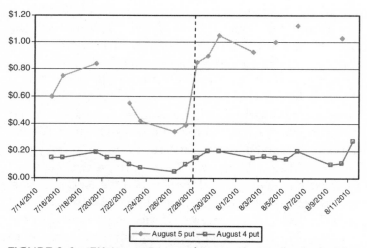

FIGURE 9.6   *EK August 5 put and August 4 put prices in the 20
trading days surrounding the earnings announcement*

Similar to the bull call spread, a carefully constructed
bear put spread can offer higher returns and lower risk
than a simple long put position. Again, the essence of the
idea is to select the spread's short leg, carefully choosing

a further-out strike price (based on a study of historical earnings announcement returns for the underlying equity) that will remain out-of-the-money. This strategy is particularly useful when the earnings announcement date is close to the option expiration date because of the fast decay of time value and the collapse of volatility after the announcement. An aggressive trader could also consider a ratio put strategy, which involves shorting more lower strike puts than those that were longed. The risk of this more aggressive strategy is the one that applies to all ratio spreads that are heavier on the short side: a black swan event, in which the negative stock price movement is much larger than was anticipated under historical scenarios. Thus, proper risk management is critical for this ratio strategy.

Easy Money?

No, not at all. As we've mentioned, we believe these directional plays are quite difficult to implement. It's true that *if* the direction is predicted correctly, the profits are dollar-for-dollar better than other strategies. But the problem is that it's unlikely that you'll be consistently correct in predicting the direction of the market reaction. We drove home that point in Chapter 6, "Market Reactions to Earnings Surprises (Are Full of Surprises)."

For instance, in the Kraft example, what if you had incorrectly predicted a bearish position on Kraft? Instead of purchasing the calls that we did in Example 9.1, we would have purchased puts. The puts would have declined in value from $0.75 on the day before the announcement to $0.27 the next day. That's a −64.0%

loss. Similarly, what if we were incorrectly bullish on Kodak? Instead of purchasing the puts as we did in Example 9.3, we would have purchased calls. The calls would have declined in value from $0.30 on the day before the announcement to $0.05 the next day. That's a −83.0% loss. Much like the gains we showed in the example, these are huge losses (and a testament to the leveraged power of options trading). And we would stress that the probability of such losses is higher than you estimate. Despite what anyone tells you, it's just very difficult to predict the short-term direction of stock prices.

Can we profit from the market reaction to an earnings announcements without forecasting the direction of the price movement? Certainly. These are the straddle or strangle strategies that we discuss in the next chapter. They represent the core trading strategy of our book.

Endnote

1. *The gaps in pricing are due to zero trading volume on those particular days.*

Chapter 10

Long Straddle and Strangle Strategies

We ended the preceding chapter by discussing how difficult it is to predict the movement of stock prices. This is in line with our detailed discussions in Chapters 5 and 6, where we presented evidence of how difficult it is to predict market reactions to earnings surprises. This chapter discusses our main solution to this issue of predicting the direction of prices. The solution is simple: Enter options positions where you simply *don't have to predict* the direction. The straddle and strangle positions we discuss in this chapter fulfill this requirement. They are volatility strategies, where we seek large movements in the stock price—without caring about the direction of this movement. These straddles represent the core strategy of our book.

The Basics of a Straddle/Strangle Strategy

How do we sidestep the issue of having to call the right direction of a stock's price movement? The answer is a straddle or strangle strategy—fairly standard and well-known approaches. We did not invent them. Our major contribution is in emphasizing their usefulness in trading around earnings announcements.

A straddle position entails buying one call and one put at the same strike price (and same expiration month). For instance, for the Eastman Kodak example from the preceding chapter, this would entail buying an August 5 put, as well as an August 5 call. The straddle largely sidesteps the issue of having to forecast the direction of stock price, because you have essentially put on bets in both directions. Specifically, if the stock price moves up, your call makes a profit, and your put loses value. If the stock price moves down, your put makes a profit, and your call loses value. All we need is for the profitable side of the trade to be *sufficiently* profitable to make up for the loss in value of the unprofitable side of the trade. What works in our favor is that the loss is capped at the original purchase price, and the gain is uncapped, and in theory has unlimited upside potential. The nature of the payoff structure and this betting-in-both-directions idea mean that the straddle strategy is a volatility trade. (All option trades are, in the end, volatility trades to some degree.) Last, we note that in terms of risk-reward profile, the long straddle position has uncapped reward potential (because one leg of the position has unlimited profit potential) and capped risk (because the worst case is both legs becoming worthless).

What makes the straddle attractive for trades surrounding the earnings announcement is that so many market reactions to earnings announcements are so large that the condition for a straddle strategy to be profitable is more likely to be satisfied than in other nonannouncement periods. These large market movements are precisely what we discussed in Chapters 5 and 6. Recall that half of the earnings announcement returns that have occurred in the past three decades are about *30 times the magnitude* of the average nonannouncement return. Now, if you cannot predict the *direction* of such large market moves, you can still profit by utilizing a straddle strategy. If the market reaction to the earnings surprise is insufficiently large, the straddle will be unprofitable. For instance, this would happen if the company made its earnings announcement and the market didn't react, with the stock price remaining stagnant. As we discuss in the next chapter, if you believe that the market reaction to the upcoming earnings announcement will be *insignificant*, you can still profit from this view by shorting the straddle. (But this presents its own set of significant risks.)

Similar to a straddle strategy, a strangle strategy also entails buying a put and a call (again with the same expiration), except not at the same strike price. Strangle trades tend to be cheaper, because both the put and call can be purchased at strike prices that are out of the money. For instance, for the Eastman Kodak example, when the stock is trading at $4.93, you may purchase an August 5 call and an August 4 put. In this case, because the stock is trading at $4.93, both the call and the put are out-of-the-money. (Unlike this strangle, a straddle trade typically requires one trade to be in-the-money. For instance, purchasing both the August 5 call and the August 5 put would mean that the call is out-of-the-money, while the put is slightly in-the-money. Sometimes, both the put and call positions may be purchased *at*-the-money, but this is only in the rare case where the stock price happens to be trading at exactly $5.)

Let's look at two examples first (Examples 10.1 and 10.2), which are related to the same earnings announcement. Example 10.1 shows the results of a straddle strategy, and Example 10.2 shows the results of a strangle strategy. You'll note that one common theme in these two examples is that the market reaction to the earnings news was fairly difficult to predict beforehand, especially given the direction of the earnings surprise that each company announced. Thus, directional bets on these particular earnings announcements were likely to be money-losing ventures even if you correctly predicted the direction of the earnings surprise. This was the main theme of Chapters 5 and 6. We illustrate that the straddle and strangle strategies are more appropriate for such cases. However, as we show in Example 10.2, these strategies are profitable only if the price movement of the underlying equity is sufficiently large.

Example 10.1: Long Straddle Position (NASDAQ: AKAM)

Here is an example of how to implement a straddle options trading strategy that takes full advantage of the price movements surrounding an earnings announcement. Consider Akamai Technologies (NASDAQ: AKAM), the largest supplier of software to make online media load faster. The company has a $6.4 billion market cap and is widely followed by the market, with 22 analysts following it, and an institutional ownership near 90%. On Wednesday, July 28, 2010, the stock was trading essentially flat for the day, at $44.03 near the close (see Figure 10.1). Earnings for the second quarter were to be announced aftermarket that day. In the 2 weeks prior to the earnings announcement, Akamai's stock price was trading roughly in the $43 to $45 range.

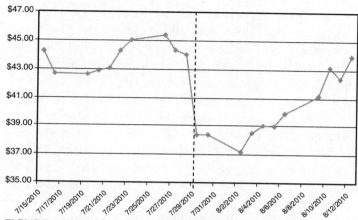

FIGURE 10.1 *Akamai Technologies (NASDAQ: AKAM) stock price in the 20 trading days surrounding the earnings announcement*

As the market closed, Akamai made its announcement around 4:30 pm. According to the *Wall Street Journal*, EPS for its second quarter was $0.34, which was completely in line with expectations. Akamai's total revenue was $245.3 million, beating analysts' revenue projections by $2 million. Since there was a zero earnings surprise, the market reaction to the earnings announcement should have been quite small, right? Well, not quite. In fact, Akamai's stock price fell by 13% the next day, despite strong revenue and earnings growth. So what's the problem? The company apparently failed to raise its third quarter estimate above analysts' prior expectations. The shares were punished, closing the following day at $38.35. (The stock closed as low as $37.20 a few days later.) How would we profit from this earnings news (or non-news) without having to predict the elusive market reaction? A simple straddle position would do the trick.

Here's how it works. On Wednesday before market close, we would open both a long call and long put position, with a $44 strike price. As we discuss in Chapter 8, "Practical Considerations Before Implementing Trades," option price movements are most sensitive to the near-month contracts, so we pick the August 44s. The August 44 put was trading at about $2.34 before market close. Let's purchase ten of these put contracts, representing a $2,340 purchase and a bet that Akamai's stock price will decline before August expiration. Next, the August 44 call was also trading at exactly $2.34, so let's also purchase ten of these contracts. This represents a $2,340 bet that Akamai's stock price will increase before August expiration. The $2.34 price for both the put and call are just a coincidence. As shown in Figure 10.2, the prices of the puts and calls fluctuated inversely in the rough range of $2.00 to $3.50. Specifically, the puts ranged from $1.80 in the few days prior to the earnings announcement to $3.60 on July 20. The calls similarly were as high as $3.19 a few days prior to the earnings announcement and had hit a low of $1.95 during the 10-day period prior to the earnings announcement.

In any case, because Akamai's stock was trading at $44.03 on the day before the earnings announcement, both the put and call positions are essentially at-the-money (but technically, the call is in-the-money, and the put is out-of-the-money). If we were to hold on to both positions until expiration, our breakeven point would be whatever the stock price is above and beyond our two option purchases. That is, with two purchases of $2.34, this is an outlay of $4.68, so we would need Akamai's stock price to move by more than this $4.68. In which direction? Because this is a straddle position, we haven't mentioned anything about the direction of the movement, because we simply *do not care* about the direction. But to be complete, let's work the numbers. For the put position to be profitable, we would need a $4.68 downward move from the $44.00 close to $39.32. Similarly, for the call position to be profitable, we would need a $4.68 upward move from the $44.00 close to $48.68.

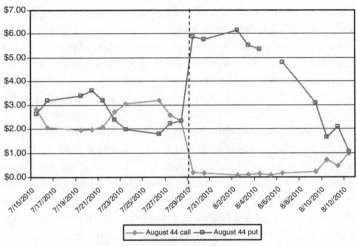

FIGURE 10.2 *AKAM August 44 put and August 44 call prices in the 20 trading days surrounding the earnings announcement*

As mentioned earlier, Akamai's stock fell 13%, to $38.35, when it announced earnings. This means that the put leg of our straddle has increased in value, while the call leg has decreased. And if we look at the threshold pricing just discussed, this $38.35 closing price definitely meets the downside threshold of $39.32. However, that is only if we were to hold till expiration, and it rarely makes sense to hold the straddle positions till expiration. In fact, there's a very compelling argument to simply close out of our positions right after a surge in volatility of the underlying stock. This is all the more true because we are always opening contracts in the near-month expiration, where the effects of time decay are particularly strong.

On Thursday, July 29 (the day after we put on our straddle position), as expected, the value of the call has decreased significantly. The August 44 call collapsed in value to $0.20, which is a 91.5% decrease. On the other hand, the value of the put has surged: the August 44 put increased in value from $2.34 to $5.86. That's a 150.4% increase in value. The increase in the value of the put far outweighs the decrease in the value of the call. This is the essence of a volatility play. If we were to close both of these positions at this point, we would have a $3,520 profit for the put position (= (5.86 − 2.34) × 100 × 10) and a $2,140 loss for the call position. This nets out to a total profit of $1,380 on an initial investment of $4,680, which is a 29.5% return in one day—*without having to predict* the direction of the earnings surprise or the even-more-unpredictable market reaction to the surprise.

Table 10.1 summarizes the Akamai profits from a long straddle.

TABLE 10.1   *Profit from a Long Straddle Position (NASDAQ: AKAM)*

	Stock Price	Long August 44 Put Price	Long August 44 Call Price	Long Straddle, August 44 Put Plus August 44 Call
July 28, 2010	$44.03	$2.34	$2.34	$4.68
July 29, 2010	$38.35	$5.86	$0.20	$6.06
$ Change	−$5.68	$3.52	−$2.14	$1.38
% Change	−12.9%	150.4%	−91.5%	29.5%

Note that if we had held our position further past the earnings announcement date, there were a few more days of momentum, as Akamai's stock price continued to descend. However, a retracement occurred in the days that followed, as apparently the initial reaction was an overreaction. For the straddle strategy, this means that holding onto the position longer would translate into a loss of profits as the underlying equity drifted back toward pre-earnings announcement prices. Additionally, we are fighting the strong forces of time decay in the final days of the soon-to-expire contract.

Last, let's take a moment to discuss the trade from the entry point. Specifically, what if we had opened the position earlier, perhaps 5 or 10 days before the earnings announcement? Many traders believe the increase in implied volatility as the earnings announcement date approaches makes long straddle strategies prohibitively expensive. The following example contradicts this common belief. During the 2 weeks prior to our entry point, the straddle cost as much as $5.58 (on July 20), and even at its cheapest point (on July 27), the price of $4.80 is still higher than our entry point. This is an example of why these common arguments do not *always* hold water. Essentially, opening a long position 2 weeks ahead of time exposes you to 2 additional weeks of time decay. Indeed, if we were to think about it from strictly a number-of-days perspective, our short-term trade is exposed to one day of time decay. The earlier entry is exposed to 5, 6, 7 days of time decay—whatever number of days you'd like to enter earlier. The argument of the gradual creeping up of implied volatility therefore must be taken in balance with the cost of time decay. To be sure, there is indeed an increase in implied volatility. On July 15, the put's volatility is 47.75, steadily increasing to 53.67

on July 28, the day before the earnings announcement (and collapsing to 43.49 upon the earnings announcement). The call's volatility is similar. However, this increase is overpowered by the time decay. This is particularly true in these types of strategies that implement the front-month expiration contracts where time decay is a particularly powerful force. Using far-out expiration months would certainly mitigate the time decay issue, but then you've sacrificed delta.

Example 10.2: Long Strangle Position (NASDAQ: AKAM)

The preceding discussion was about a profitable straddle position, where both the put and call positions were placed (very close to) at-the-money. Another possibility, where we would essentially be betting on even larger volatility on earnings announcement day, is the strangle position. As mentioned earlier, the strangle differs from the straddle insofar as we open both the put and call positions at out-of-the-money strike prices. For instance, for the same Akamai trade, let's try opening into a strangle with strike prices that are $2 out of the money. For the put position, we can open the August 42 put for $1.52. Ten contracts of this downside bet would cost us $1,520. Similarly, an August 46 call position was priced at $1.43 right before the earnings announcement. Ten contracts of this upside bet would cost $1,430. The total cash outlay is then $2,950. Note that the strangle is cheaper than the straddle. This makes sense, because both the put and call are purchased out-of-the-money.

Upon the earnings announcement, the call closed the following day at $0.08 (see Figure 10.3), which is a $1.35/contract loss, or $1,350. However, the put increased in value to $4.06, which is a $2.54/contract gain, or $2,540. Together, this is a total net gain of $1,190 on an initial investment of $3,050. This translates into a 40.3% gain. This higher return makes sense, because the positions were placed out-of-the-money and therefore required a larger underlying equity price movement for the positions to get in-the-money. However, we stress here that because our goal is to exploit *short-term* price movements, we are not as concerned with whether the option contracts actually *expire* in- or out-of-the-money. We only need prices to have a large movement, either up or down. To the extent that strangles are placed with strike prices that are very out-of-the-money, this is a riskier volatility play, because it requires a larger movement in stock price. However, also note that the implied volatility of the options with further-out strike prices is lower relative to those with close-to-the-money strike prices. These differences in implied volatilities can have a significant impact on the prices of the options you purchase.

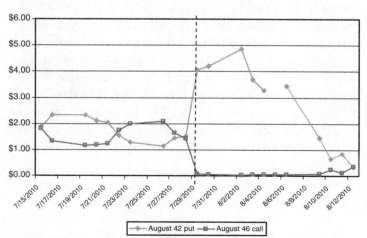

FIGURE 10.3 *AKAM August 42 put and August 46 call prices in the 20 trading days surrounding the earnings announcement*

Table 10.2 summarizes the Akamai profits from a long strangle.

TABLE 10.2   *Profit from a Long Strangle Position (NASDAQ: AKAM)*

	Stock Price	Long August 42 Put Price	Long August 46 Call Price	Long Strangle, August 42 Put Plus August 46 Call
July 28, 2010	$44.03	$1.52	$1.43	$2.95
July 29, 2010	$38.35	$4.06	$0.08	$4.14
$ Change	–$5.68	$2.54	–$1.35	$1.19
% Change	–12.9%	167.1%	–94.4%	40.3%

Last, let's talk about different exit and entry points. If you continued to hold onto this strangle position past its earnings announcement day, note the similar decline in the value of the put option. This is particularly the case as the August 42 put actually becomes out-of-the-money in the final days of the contract, as Akamai's stock price climbs to almost $44. For earlier entry points, much like the previous discussion of the straddle position, earlier entry points for each of the 10 days before the earnings announcement date are all more expensive than the day-before entry point we selected. Specifically, the highest price of this strangle is on July 15 (the first day of our chart), with a price of $3.71. It steadily marches downward—time decay at work—till our July 28 entry point, where we purchased our strangle for $2.95.

Example 10.3: Long Straddle Position (NASDAQ: GENZ)

Here is an example that again highlights the difficulty of predicting the direction of the market's reaction to earnings surprises and shows why the straddle works perfectly for us. Genzyme is a biotechnology company whose product and service portfolio is focused on rare genetic disease disorders, renal diseases, orthopedics, cancer, transplants, and immune disease. It has a market capitalization of roughly $17 billion and is followed by 20 analysts. On July 20, 2010, a day before their earnings announcement for the second quarter, its stock price closed at $52.26 (see Figure 10.4). Going into the earnings announcement, the consensus forecast was an EPS of $0.51. Unfortunately, on July 21, the company announced a severe miss. Genzyme's actual reported earnings were only $0.18 per share, which is a −64% miss from the expected $0.51 per share. This negative result was attributed to a few factors, including charges for discarded drug material, plant shutdowns, and a write-down of an investment in Isis Pharmaceuticals. Moreover, Genzyme reported total revenue of $1.08 billion, missing analysts' revenue projections of $1.16 billion. On top of the negative earnings and revenue surprises, Genzyme lowered its earnings and revenue guidance for 2010 due to persistent drug supply problems. The company now projected adjusted EPS in the range of $1.90 to $2.00 and total revenue in the range of $4.4 billion to $4.5 billion for 2010. Analysts' EPS and revenue expectations were both higher, at $2.47 and $4.95 billion, respectively.

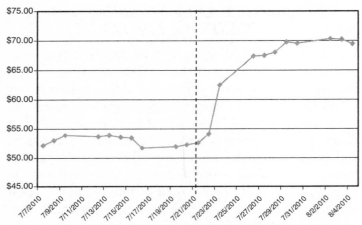

FIGURE 10.4   *Genzyme (NASDAQ: GENZ) stock price in the 20 trading days surrounding the earnings announcement*

Given all the bad news, Genzyme's stock price should have dropped like a stone, right? Well, its price actually closed at a *higher* $52.62. At one point during the trading day, it reached as high as $54.37. (As you read the price chart, note that this is 2 days *before* the big price movement you see. We talk about this in a moment.)

This example brings up several points. The first is to reiterate that earnings surprises do not necessarily help us predict market reactions. Genzyme clearly missed consensus estimates and provided worse-than-expected guidance for the future, and yet the stock price barely moved. In fact, it actually went (slightly) in the opposite direction. If we had made a directional bearish play on this by purchasing put options—and given the dire news, that would seem to be the right play—we would have lost quite a bit of money. We would have bought the August $52.50 put

on the day before the announcement for $2.25. By the end
of the next day, the put option lost 35.6% of its value,
closing the day at $1.45 (see Figure 10.5).

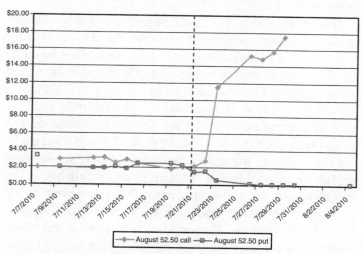

FIGURE 10.5   *GENZ August 52.50 put and August 52.50 call
prices in the 20 trading days surrounding the earnings announcement*

The second point to make is that, because the stock
price barely moved, a long straddle play would not have
been profitable here either. Assume that we purchased
the puts for the aforementioned $2.25 and also pur-
chased call options (at the same strike and expiration),
which would have cost $2.10. This is a total purchase
price of $4.35. On the day of the announcement, the
puts were worth $1.45, and the calls increased a bit to
$2.20. That means our combined position is now worth
$3.65. Compared to our purchase price, this is a $0.70
loss, representing a 16.1% erosion of our position. Even

if we had tried to purchase the straddle during the 2 weeks prior to the earnings announcement, our entry price never would have been better; at its peak, the straddle would have cost $5.30 on July 7.

The reason that the straddle is unprofitable in this example is that the small price movement only slightly increases the value of one side of the straddle (the call). At the same time, the value of the other side (the put) decreases significantly because of the volatility collapse. Volatility collapse is triggered by disclosures, such as earnings announcements, that significantly deflate the uncertainty about a stock that existed when approaching the earnings announcement date. What separates a profitable straddle trade from an unprofitable one is the magnitude of the underlying equity's price movement. If the stock's movement is sufficiently large, the winning side of the straddle almost always makes much more profit than the loss incurred by the losing side. On the other hand, if the price movement is small, the loss incurred by the losing side often outweighs the profit by the winning side because of volatility collapse.

Another aspect of this discussion, then, is the idea of not overpaying for the puts and calls with respect to their implied volatilities. When the implied volatility of a certain strike price is high, by definition the potential of a large stock price movement is already priced into it, which makes it all the more difficult for that leg of the straddle to be profitable.

The last point we'll make for this particular trade— and we've been saving it till the end—is the dramatic spike in price in the few days after the earnings announcement. Is this a delayed reaction to some good news that was buried in the earnings press release? Hardly. A few days later, it was revealed that Genzyme was the target of a potential buyout bid from the French biotech company Sanofi-Aventis. This unanticipated news caused Genzyme's stock price to spike, as it did for the call options. Here is an example of a bad trade that frankly just got lucky. The non-news of the earnings announcement caused the long straddle position to lose value. An astute trader would close this position not only because no stock price bounce occurred for the anticipated event, but because of the ever-growing time decay that occurs for front-month contracts. If for some reason you had decided to stay with the trade (although at the time we would have been hard-pressed to give a reason for continuing the trade after earnings had been announced) the straddle would have been very profitable. In our view, the buyout announcement further highlights the advantage of earnings announcements: their regular, recurring, anticipated nature. We talk about this in the next chapter, but a *short* straddle here would have been devastating to our portfolio.

Table 10.3 summarizes the Genzyme losses from a long straddle.

TABLE 10.3   *Loss from a Long Straddle Position (NASDAQ: GENZ)*

	Stock Price	Long August 52.50 Put Price	Long August 52.50 Call Price	Long Straddle, August 52.50 Put Plus August 52.50 Call
July 20, 2010	$52.26	$2.25	$2.10	$4.35
July 21, 2010	$52.62	$1.45	$2.20	$3.65
$ Change	–$5.68	–$0.80	$0.10	–$0.70
% Change	–12.9%	–35.6%	4.8%	–16.1%

Example 10.4: Long Straddle Position (NYSE: EK)

To further illustrate the potential profitability—as well as potential losses—of straddle positions, we next revisit two of the directional positions we entered into in the preceding chapter. First, we discuss a straddle on Eastman Kodak, a profitable trade. Then we discuss a similar straddle on Kraft Foods—this time, an unprofitable trade.

Recall that we opened a long put position for Eastman Kodak due to our bearish views. However, if we were concerned about an unpredictable market reaction, we might make a bet on volatility instead, using a straddle position. To do so, we would simply add a long call position to our long put position. As before, the August 5 put costs $0.39 before the announcement (see Figure 10.6). Buying an August 5 call would cost an additional $0.30, making our total cost for the straddle $0.69. Upon the earnings announcement, the next day, we've already discussed the increase in price of the put to $0.85. However, the straddle position means that if our put position increased in price, our call position very likely decreased in price. The call price in fact decreased to $0.05. This means that the new value of our straddle after the earnings announcement is $0.90 (= 0.85 + 0.05). This represents a total profit of $0.21, or 30.4% on our straddle position. This straddle is, by definition, not as profitable as a pure directional bet of purchasing only the put. However, it reduces the risk of losses because we have essentially hedged the trade's directional nature.

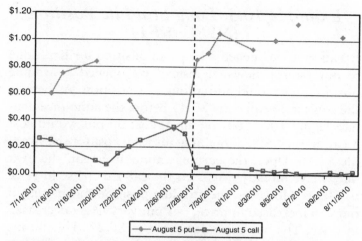

FIGURE 10.6   *EK August 5 put and August 5 call prices in the 20 trading days surrounding the earnings announcement*

Table 10.4 summarizes the Kodak profits from a long straddle.

TABLE 10.4   *Profit from a Long Straddle Position (NYSE: EK)*

	Stock Price	Long August 5 Put Price	Long August 5 Call Price	Long Straddle, August 5 Put Plus August 5 Call
July 27, 2010	$4.93	$0.39	$0.30	$0.69
July 28, 2010	$4.18	$0.85	$0.05	$0.90
$ Change	−$0.75	$0.46	−$0.25	$0.21
% Change	−15.2%	117.9%	−83.3%	30.4%

Example 10.5: Long Straddle Position (NYSE: KFT)

Recall that we opened a long call position for Kraft due to our bullish views. If instead we opened a straddle position, we would add a long put position. As before, the August 30 call costs $0.41 before the announcement (see Figure 10.7). Buying an August 30 put would cost an additional $0.75, making our total cost for the straddle $1.16. Upon the earnings announcement, the next day, we've already discussed the call's increase in price to $0.66. However, the straddle position means that if our call increased in price, our put very likely decreased in price. The put price decreased to $0.27. This means that the new value of our straddle after the earnings announcement is $0.93 (= 0.27 + 0.66). That represents a total loss of –$0.23, or –19.8% on our straddle position. This is therefore another case where the price of the underlying equity security did not swing wildly enough for our option position to become profitable; after all, the straddle is a bet on volatility. Moreover, the volatility collapse further eroded the value of our positions. For instance, the put's implied volatility had been hovering in the 18 to 19 range in the week before the earnings announcement. On the day before the earnings announcement, August 5, it spiked to 23.66. However, the following day, implied volatility again fell to 18.32. The call option exhibited a similar pattern in implied volatility.

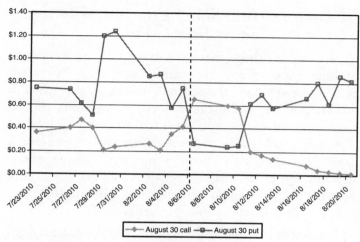

FIGURE 10.7 *KFT August 30 put and August 30 call prices in the 20 trading days surrounding the earnings announcement*

Table 10.5 summarizes the Kraft losses from a long straddle.

TABLE 10.5 *Loss from a Long Straddle Position (NYSE: KFT)*

	Stock Price	Long August 30 Put Price	Long August 30 Call Price	Long Straddle, August 30 Put Plus August 30 Call
August 5, 2010	$29.66	$0.75	$0.41	$1.16
August 6, 2010	$30.36	$0.27	$0.66	$0.93
$ Change	$0.70	–$0.48	$0.25	–$0.23
% Change	2.4%	–64.0%	60.9%	–19.8%

Example 10.6: Short Iron Butterfly and Short Iron Condor

As we discuss throughout the book, we prefer simple options strategies over complex ones. In many ways, we believe the straddle and strangle positions described in this chapter can fulfill the majority of volatility-related positions that you would want to enter into, at least as they relate to trades around earnings announcement days. However, let's spend a moment talking about another type of trade, because we've essentially described all its components already. This option position is called the short iron butterfly.

The short iron butterfly is essentially a straddle position that is a combination of the bull call spread and bear put spread that we discussed in the preceding chapter. What this means is that we continue to open a long straddle position but also open short positions for the put and call at further-out strike prices. For instance, for the case of Genzyme (Example 10.3), we had originally opened a straddle for the August 52.50 by longing the August 52.50 call, as well as the August 52.50 put. To implement a short iron butterfly position, in addition to this straddle, we would then sell short the outer strike prices. Specifically, this would entail simultaneously selling short the August 55 call and selling short the August 50 put. At the time of the original trade (July 20, 2010), the August 55 call was priced at $1.10, and the August 50 put was priced at $1.25. Because you would sell these contracts short, you would essentially collect a premium of $2.35. This premium brings down the net cost of your straddle, which you purchased for $4.35, to a net $2.00 (refer to Table 10.3). The following day, when the value of your long straddle decreased to $3.65, the value of the outer strike price options you sold also decreased to $2.15 (that's $1.55 for the short call and $0.60 for the short put). If you were to close the entire position that day, you would essentially have a $0.20 profit from the outer strike prices, because you would be buying back at $2.15 something you had sold short for $2.35 the previous day. In the case of this Genzyme trade, this means that your original loss of –$0.70 from the long straddle is reduced by $0.20 to –$0.50.

Thus, the short positions of your short iron butterfly can reduce the cost and potential losses of your long straddle. However, because you are short the outer strike prices, you are essentially capping the otherwise unlimited potential upside of a straddle. For instance, in the case of Genzyme, if the underlying equity price had tanked to, say, $45, under the original straddle scenario, your long August 52.50 put would recognize the full benefit of this freefall in stock price. However, with a short iron butterfly, you've essentially limited the benefit of this freefall. Although our long put recognizes the benefit of stock price movement from $52.50 to $50, any further down movement in the stock price is neutralized by the short August 50 put. Essentially, when the stock price moves lower than $50, any gains you have in the long August 52.50 put are wiped out by the losses you have from the short August 50 put. Last, in such a case, the price of your short August 55 call will further decrease, which is a profit to you.

Whether you believe the reduction in cost from the short positions is worth limiting profit potential from the long positions is a personal choice you must consider. Our view is that these types of more-complex trades are rarely worth the effort. Here we have four different legs, four different bid-ask spreads that we must fight against, and fourfold transaction costs.

Last, the short iron condor is essentially the same type of position as the short iron butterfly, except that instead of a long straddle, we are opening a long strangle. Example 10.2 and Table 10.2 for the Akamai strangle are examples of this. Specifically, in the Akamai example, the long strangle was opened by longing the August 46 call and longing the August 42 put (while the stock price was at $44.03). To create a short iron condor position, we would simply sell short outer strikes again. For instance, we would sell short the August 47 call and the August 41 put.

Chapter 11

Short Straddle and Strangle Strategies

In the preceding chapter, we laid out the basic details of our main trading strategy, the longing of straddles and strangles near earnings announcement dates. To give you a balanced view, we made sure to include some losing trades alongside the winning ones. However, we fear that you might be eager to see profits in *all* your trades. You might have taken note of the losing trades as ones where you could have simply *shorted* the positions instead of longing them. That would turn the losing trades into winners. This chapter reviews the pros and cons of such shorting strategies. These are not trades that we necessarily recommend, but we believe there's plenty to learn from analyzing them.

Making a Case for the Short

We described six different examples in the preceding chapter. Some were winning trades, and some were losers:

- Akamai straddle: 29.5% gain
- Akamai strangle: 40.3% gain

- Genzyme straddle: –16.1% loss
- Kodak straddle: 30.4% gain
- Kraft straddle: –19.8% loss
- Genzyme short iron butterfly: –25% loss

For the three losing trades, any investor/trader who is familiar with selling short could tell you that you could have had a gain instead of a loss on these long positions by simply going short the positions instead. That is the subject of this chapter. We stress, however, that this is a risky strategy that goes against much of the economic intuition that we have been building in this book— namely, the large, unpredictable market reactions around earnings announcements. Nonetheless, plenty can be learned from discussing the issues.

We have presented essentially three core empirical findings in this book. First, earnings surprises are common and plentiful (Chapter 4). Second, the market reactions to these earnings surprises can be significant (Chapter 5). Last, the direction of the market reactions is incredibly difficult to predict, even if we have perfect foresight into the direction of the earnings surprise (Chapter 6). We believe these findings are strong evidence that supports our main view that plenty of money can be made in longing straddles and strangles.

The flip side of this argument is that plenty of money can be lost in *shorting* straddles/strangles. However, a case can be made that perhaps such shorting strategies can actually be profitable. Here is the argument. Four decades ago, Ball and Brown (1968) published a now-very-famous study that found that stock prices tended to steadily run up several months before good earnings numbers were actually reported. Similarly, stock prices tended to steadily trail downward several months before bad earnings were announced. In some ways, this finding should not be that surprising. The market is incredibly adept at detecting good and bad news pre-emptively, sniffing out information in obscure corners of the world. That's because the market is composed of a host of different types of participants—individual investors, institutional investors, analysts, lenders. They all spend time and resources trying to gather information and stay ahead of the game. They gather and analyze historical numbers from past financial statements, visit the company, and talk to key players such as management, employees, and competitors. So perhaps it's no wonder that the authors found the steady drift of prices toward the direction of a company's earnings surprise.

Suppose we were to take this argument to its *extreme*. This would imply that after the company announced its earnings, the market would have already fully anticipated this through its diligent detective work. Therefore, the market would have fully impounded the information into the stock price, such that there was really *no* reaction to the earnings announcement. The idea of no market reaction to the earnings announcement is a strong and direct contradiction of the evidence that has been mounting in the previous chapters.[1] But the point is that we would have to take the argument to the extreme for there to be no reaction. Nonetheless, this idea that the market has already anticipated a large portion of the earnings news is one of the key arguments *for* shorting straddles and strangles around earnings announcement days. The other key argument is that short straddles opened before earnings announcement dates exploit the significant increase in implied volatility around such dates and the subsequent collapse of volatility in the aftermath of the announcement when uncertainty is largely resolved. Typically, such short positions also have the added fact that time decay is working *in their favor*, but because our positions are held for fairly short periods, this is less of a point to highlight here. In essence, in the same way that a long straddle was a bet that volatility in the stock price would increase, a short straddle position is one where we are betting that volatility will *decrease*. In the perfect scenario, the stock price would remain stagnant, or trade within a narrow range, allowing both the short put and short call to expire worthless.

Let's get to some examples.

Example 11.1: Short Straddle Position (NYSE: KFT)

In the first example, to illustrate a profitable short straddle, we simply reverse the positions we opened for the Kraft straddle example discussed in the preceding chapter (Example 10.5). All the prices are the same as those found in that example and in Table 10.5; only the logic is reversed. Specifically, we would open the position by selling the August 30 put for $0.75 and the August 30 call for $0.41 (see Figure 11.1). This would result in collecting a premium of $1.16. Upon Kraft's earnings announcement, the put's price decreases to $0.27, and the call's price increases to $0.66, making the straddle now worth $0.93. This is a $0.23 decrease in price, and we would thus close the position at this price. The $0.23 therefore would be the gain from the transaction.

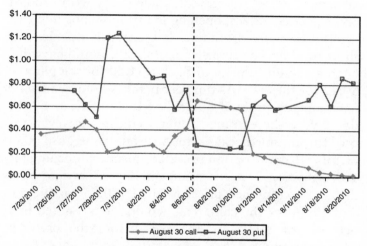

FIGURE 11.1 *KFT August 30 put and August 30 call prices in the 20 trading days surrounding the earnings announcement*

This short straddle was profitable for at least three reasons, which we list in order of importance or magnitude. First, the price of the underlying equity security did not change enough for either of our short positions to sufficiently increase in value. Second, the implied volatility priced into each leg before the earnings announcement has diminished in the aftermath (volatility collapse). Specifically, for the put option, implied volatility fell from 23.66 to 18.32 in one day. The call option's implied volatility fell from 22.68 to 18.66. Last, one day's worth of time decay has further helped our cause.

The final issue is alternative entry points. Unlike the prior *long* straddles we've discussed, because we are now the seller of the straddle, time decay works in our favor. To that extent, opening the straddle position earlier can be more profitable. For instance, opening the short straddle 5 days earlier, on July 29, would have dictated a combined price of $1.41 ($1.20 for the put and $0.21 for the call). As time decay takes hold, we would have already profited $0.25 (= $1.41 − $1.16) by the day before the earnings announcement. However, the profit from time decay is not a certainty, because other factors affect the option price. For instance, opening the short position 2 weeks prior, on July 23, would have dictated a combined price of $1.11 ($0.75 for the put and $0.36 for the call). This would have resulted in a net loss of $0.05 by the day before the earnings announcement.

Table 11.1 summarizes the Kraft gains.

TABLE 11.1   *Gain from a Short Straddle Position (NYSE: KFT)*

	Stock Price	Short August 30 Put Price	Short August 30 Call Price	Short Straddle, August 30 Put Plus August 30 Call
August 5, 2010	$29.66	$0.75	$0.41	$1.16
August 6, 2010	$30.36	$0.27	$0.66	$0.93
$ Change	$0.70	$0.48	−$0.25	$0.23
% Change	2.4%	64.0%	−60.9%	19.8%

Example 11.2: Short Straddle Position (NASDAQ: WYNN)

Our next example is of Wynn Resorts (NASDAQ: WYNN), a developer, owner, and operator of destination casino resorts, including Wynn Las Vegas and Wynn Macau. This is an example of a company that announced a very large positive earnings surprise, yet there was very little stock price reaction. At first blush, this type of muted response (where the stock price essentially remained flat) would be considered perfect for a short straddle/strangle position. But we'll illustrate here that this isn't necessarily the case in such short-term trades.

During the economic boom, Wynn Resorts' stock fetched as much as $150 per share. But the 2008 financial crisis crushed the stock, which fell almost 90% from its peak to about $15 per share. Then, with the economic recovery, the stock rebounded strongly from its March 2009 low. On July 28, 2010, the day before Wynn's earnings announcement for its second fiscal quarter, the stock closed at $87.87, a bit shy of a 500% gain from its March 2009 low (see Figure 11.2). In the 2 weeks prior to the earnings announcement, the stock price had been drifting upward from the low $80s. On the day before earnings were announced, the analyst consensus EPS estimate was $0.42 per share. On that day, the August 90 calls closed at a price of $3.15, and the August 90 puts closed at $5.73. If we were to open a short position in both, we would collect a premium of $8.88.

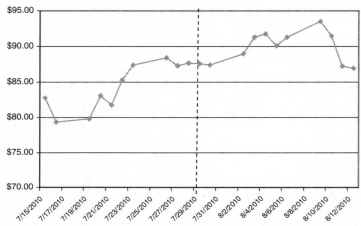

FIGURE 11.2 *Wynn Resorts (NASDAQ: WYNN) stock price in the 20 trading days surrounding the earnings announcement*

The next day, July 29, Wynn announced earnings that blew past consensus expectations. It announced actual EPS of $0.52, which was 23.8% higher than the expected $0.42. Its stock price fluctuated wildly during the day, reaching as high as $89.56 and as low as $86.09, representing as much as a 4% swing in stock price. However, it eventually closed the day, settling at $87.85, virtually unchanged from the $87.87 from the previous day. The calls closed the day at $3.10, only $0.05 off from the previous day's $3.15. The puts closed at $5.54, only a few cents off from the previous day's $5.73 (see Figure 11.3). Together, the call and put were worth $8.64 at the end of the day, a $0.24 decline from the original $8.88, representing only a 2.7% decline. The short straddle position therefore was profitable, but we gained only a net $0.24, or 2.7%, the type of profit that is very easily wiped out by transaction costs. Given the fact that Wynn's stock price had barely changed from its close of the previous day, this meager profit of $0.24 is quite disappointing. One contributing factor to these meager returns is the fact that the stock price was quite volatile on the day of the earnings announcement. This suggests that the collapse in volatility that typically is hoped for after an earnings announcement was fairly small. (Even if we had closed our position at the day's high, our call traded at $4.00, and our put traded at $4.60. This made our total position worth only $8.60, a gain of $0.28. Similarly, if we had closed our position at the day's low, our call would have traded at $2.42, and our put would have traded at $6.80, making our total position worth $9.22, a loss of $0.34.) Indeed, the implied volatility for the put was 49.38 on July 28 and fell to only 48.01 the following day, a 2.8% decrease in volatility. Similarly, the call's implied volatility went from 48.36 to 47.43 during this period.

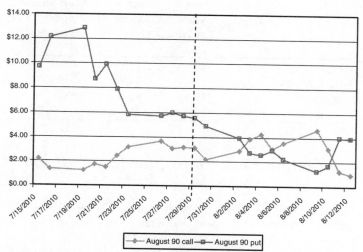

FIGURE 11.3 *WYNN August 90 call and August 90 put prices in the 20 trading days surrounding the earnings announcement*

Short straddle positions opened earlier would have been more profitable here. At its high point on July 19, the straddle was worth $14.13 (with the calls worth $1.28 and the puts worth $12.85), when the stock price closed the day at $79.80. Of course, timing this best-case scenario is difficult, but even a rule of thumb of 2 weeks prior to the earnings announcement would have fetched an $11.90 price on July 15. As for exits, as time decay took hold, you can see that the straddle steadily lost value over the next 2 weeks, closing on August 12 at a value of $4.90 when the stock was trading at $86.93. The out-of-the-money calls were priced at $1.00, and the in-the-money puts were priced at $3.90.

Table 11.2 summarizes the Wynn Resorts gains.

TABLE 11.2   *A Small Gain from a Short Straddle Position (NASDAQ: WYNN)*

	Stock Price	Short August 90 Put Price	Short August 90 Call Price	Short Straddle, August 90 Put Plus August 90 Call
July 28, 2010	$87.87	$5.73	$3.15	$8.88
July 29, 2010	$87.85	$5.54	$3.10	$8.64
$ Change	–$0.02	$0.19	$0.05	$0.24
% Change	0.0%	3.3%	1.6%	2.7%

Example 11.3: Short Straddle Position (NASDAQ: WFMI)

Whole Foods Market owns and operates a chain of 284 natural and organic foods supermarkets, mostly in the U.S., but also in Canada and the UK. Let's look at an example of how Whole Foods' earnings announcement, relatively mundane on the surface, wreaked havoc on its stock price—and how we could have gotten burned in a short straddle position. On August 3, 2010, WFMI closed the day at $39.49 (see Figure 11.4). During the 2 weeks prior to this date, the stock had been swinging between a low of $36.31 and a high of $40.15. The consensus estimate for its third quarter of 2010 was $0.38 a share, which would represent a near doubling of earnings from a year ago, and the third consecutive quarter of revenue increases. At the time, before its earnings announcement, WFMI's August 40 calls cost $1.40 per share, and the August 40 puts cost $1.96 per share. Its prices were also trading in a fairly wide range.

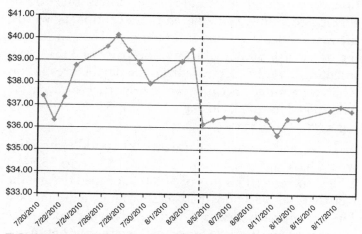

FIGURE 11.4 *Whole Foods Market (NASDAQ: WFMI) stock price in the 20 trading days surrounding the earnings announcement*

After market close on that day, WFMI announced that it had exactly met earnings expectations, clocking a $0.38 EPS for the quarter. Moreover, it had beaten estimates of revenues, booking $2.2 billion in revenue, which was higher than the expected $2.1 billion. Because WFMI just met earnings expectations, on the surface, this sounds like a perfect trade for a short straddle position (or perhaps a long call position due to the positive revenue surprise).[2] The short straddle would mean we collect a premium of $3.36.

So how did this trade play out? Well, the market reacted very negatively. The following day, August 4, WFMI closed down −8.4%, at $36.16. What happened? Apparently, in Whole Foods' earnings announcement, mixed in with its glowing report of how it met current earnings and beat revenue expectations were some cautionary words about future expectations due to the slowing economy. Hanging on those cautionary words, the market decided to have a field day. The calls closed the day worth $0.06, which is a decrease of $1.34, representing a 95.7% decrease from the day before. This is what we wanted, because we are short. However, the puts spiked in value, closing the day at $3.90, representing a 98.9% increase.

If we had shorted the August 40 straddle, its price would have increased from its original $3.36 to $3.96, a 17.8% increase. This loss of $0.60 happened despite the fact that Whole Foods had met earnings expectations. The key problem here is that the underlying stock price had moved significantly lower, making the put option we shorted significantly in-the-money. Moreover, the potential volatility collapse we had hoped for in the period after the earnings announcement did not occur because of the new uncertainty that was introduced into the market with Whole Foods' statements. This example highlights the inherent danger in trying to exploit potential volatility collapse around earnings announcements.

Specifically, although it is possible that the implied volatility embedded in each leg of the straddle will decrease in the period after the earnings announcement, it's also very possible that the implied volatility will significantly increase. It all depends on the type of news that is released and how the market interprets it.

Opening this short position on any day in the 2 weeks prior to our original entry date would have lessened the pain. One week prior, we would have gotten $3.72 for selling the straddle (see Figure 11.5). Two weeks prior, we would have gotten a hefty $4.62. In this example, time decay was again a dominant force in the position. In the period after the earnings announcement, the price of the straddle swung back and forth. For instance, even in the following day, August 5, the straddle decreased in price to $3.23, which would have allowed us to close the position at a profit. However, a few days later, on August 11, the price increased to $4.36 as the stock briefly dipped below the $36 threshold.

Table 11.3 summarizes the Whole Foods Market losses.

TABLE 11.3 *A Loss from a Short Straddle Position (NASDAQ: WFMI)*

	Stock Price	Short August 40 Put Price	Short August 40 Call Price	Short Straddle, August 40 Put Plus August 40 Call
August 3, 2010	$39.49	$1.96	$1.40	$3.36
August 4, 2010	$36.16	$3.90	$0.06	$3.96
$ Change	–$3.33	–$1.94	$1.34	–$0.60
% Change	–8.4%	–98.9%	95.7%	–17.8%

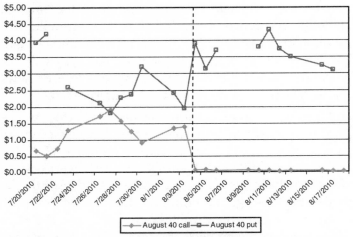

FIGURE 11.5   *WFMI August 40 call and August 40 put prices in the 20 trading days surrounding the earnings announcement*

This discussion warns against opening short straddle or short strangle positions. In terms of risk-reward profile, the short straddle offers a limited amount of upside (essentially the full amount of the premium). However, it offers an unlimited amount of downside, because large changes in price can wreak havoc on the position and can easily eat into any profits you may collect from the position's profitable leg. It is therefore possible for you to consistently collect small premiums from this short straddle strategy for quite some time, until one day you are met with one bad blowup where prices move drastically. This type of drastic movement—the so-called black swan—can easily wipe out your profits from prior gains. We believe these risks and the potentially large downsides make the appeal of exploiting volatility collapse relatively small.

Endnotes

1. *The two findings may seem a bit contradictory at first. However, it's completely possible that the market can anticipate a portion of the earnings news throughout the year and yet still be surprised when earnings are announced. This can happen because the market anticipated only a* portion, *not the entirety, of earnings news.*

2. *Revenue and expense surprises are covered in Chapter 13, "Revenue and Expense Surprises."*

Part V

Fine Tuning: Improving the Odds of a Profitable Trade

In Part IV, we presented several real examples of our main options-trading strategies, making sure to show both profitable and unprofitable trades. Part V discusses several other empirical findings from research studies that, when applied properly, will help improve your odds of making profitable trades around earnings announcements. **Chapter 12** discusses how growth companies are particularly susceptible to large downward swings when earnings are missed. **Chapter 13** describes companies that consistently and persistently beat earnings expectations. **Chapter 14** discusses revenue and expense surprises. **Chapter 15** wraps up the book with a general discussion of other empirical findings that will help further fine-tune how you think about and select your trades.

Chapter 12

Growth Expectations and the Torpedo Effect

Often, analysts refer to companies as either growth companies or value companies. Growth companies have very high expectations for future growth, and value companies have relatively lower growth. In a study by Skinner and Sloan (2002), the authors thought growth expectations might have a significant effect on how the market reacts to a company's earnings surprises. To test this possibility, the authors examined the market's reaction to more than 100,000 earnings surprises over a period starting 12 days before fiscal quarter end and ending one day after the quarter's earnings announcement. This period encompassed both the earnings surprise and almost all earnings preannouncements. They then divided the world between growth companies and value companies. (Growth expectations were measured using the company's market-to-book ratio. High market-to-book companies were considered growth companies, and low market-to-book companies were considered value companies.)

The Skinner and Sloan study yielded two important insights. First, the authors found that, given the same magnitude of earnings surprise, the market tended to react more strongly to the earnings surprises of growth companies and relatively less strongly to those of value companies. This stronger reaction was true whether they examined negative or positive earnings surprises. Either way, the reaction was stronger for growth companies and weaker for value companies.

The second insight of their study was the *symmetry* and *asymmetry* in the market reactions. Specifically, for value companies, they found that the market tended to react to both positive and negative earnings surprises about evenly. On average, when a value company announced earnings, the market reaction to bad earnings news was about the same magnitude as it would be for good earnings news. In other words, the response to both good news and bad news displayed *symmetry*. On the other hand, growth companies displayed asymmetry in the response. Specifically, for growth companies, the authors found that the market's reaction to bad earnings news was much more severe than its reaction to similar good earnings news. Put simply, for growth companies, the market tended to punish bad earnings news much more strongly than it rewarded good earnings news— that's the *asymmetry*. Because of this severe negative market reaction to bad earnings news, this phenomenon has been nicknamed the *torpedo effect*. A seemingly small miss of earnings can have a devastating effect on a growth company's stock price. This doesn't mean that growth companies will always be punished severely, or that value companies will not be punished severely, but we can make statements about what happens on average.

What are the implications of these findings for options traders in tune with earnings announcements? First, because the average magnitude of the market reaction is larger for growth stocks, this suggests that potentially larger gains can be reaped from a long straddle strategy for growth stocks (relative to value stocks). Second, the gains from the strategy will be particularly profitable if the growth company has negative earnings news. This suggests that a long *ratio* straddle strategy, with a bias on the put side (for instance, a 2-to-1 ratio of puts to calls), may be more appropriate for growth stocks.

Example 12.1: Torpedo Effect for a Small Earnings Miss (NYSE: BHI)

Our first example of the torpedo effect is Baker Hughes (NYSE: BHI). Baker Hughes is engaged in the oil field services industry, supplying drilling/consulting/reservoir products and technology services and systems to the worldwide oil and natural gas industry. Baker Hughes has a market cap of $17 billion and has a very high P/E ratio of over 40, which is in the range of a growth company. Indeed, the company's total revenues and earnings in 2008 had doubled those of 2005, increasing every year in this period. The company's 2009 revenue and profits were lower than those of 2008, but the fast growth resumed in the third quarter of 2009.

On August 2, 2010, the day before BHI announced its earnings for its second fiscal quarter, its stock price closed at $50.23 (see Figure 12.1). In the weeks leading up to the earnings announcement, the stock had been trading in the range of $48 to $50. Before the earnings announcement, BHI's August 50 call closed at $2.09, and the same strike/month put closed at $1.88. A straddle position therefore would cost $3.97 total. If we purchased five contracts of each, that would be a total cost of $1,985.

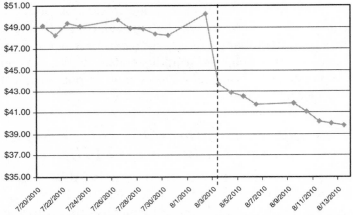

FIGURE 12.1   *Baker Hughes (NYSE: BHI) stock price in the 20 trading days surrounding the earnings announcement*

Consensus estimates were $0.43 per share. The next day, earnings of $0.41 per share were announced, so Baker Hughes missed expectations by a mere $0.02. The stock's performance after the disappointing earnings announcement closely resembled a ship hit by a torpedo: the stock tumbled 13% and closed at $43.66. This one-day loss was the steepest since December 2008. It was conjectured that Baker Hughes' falling margins in Latin America and Africa was the reason behind the brutal sell-off.

Upon close the next day, the call dwindled in value to $0.06, losing virtually all its value. However, the put exploded in value to $6.33, a 236.7% increase (see Figure 12.2). Together, the straddle had a new value of $6.39, which represents a $2.42 gain from the original $3.97 investment, making it a hefty 60.9% gain. This is a classic example of how to exploit the torpedo effect that occurs from small misses in earnings by using a direction-neutral straddle position. Next, let's consider a similar torpedo effect from a small miss in revenues.

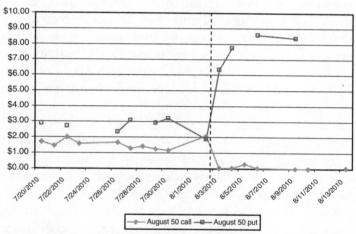

FIGURE 12.2   *BHI August 50 call and August 50 put prices in the 20 trading days surrounding the earnings announcement*

Example 12.2: Torpedo Effect for a Small Revenue Miss (NASDAQ: NFLX)

In this example, we discuss a fast-growing company that you've almost certainly heard of: Netflix. In the current trading environment, where people fear double-dip recession, deflation, and other monsters, much tension has resulted over how companies are maintaining topline revenue growth. Because of this, particular attention is being paid to *how* these earnings surprises are generated—through cuts in expenses or a rise in revenues. Thus, this torpedo effect in growth companies can be particularly acute with misses of revenues.

Consider the recent case of Netflix (NASDAQ: NFLX), a subscription service that streams movies and television episodes over the Internet and sends DVDs by mail. Ten years ago, Netflix was an obscure company that was quietly revolutionizing how people access entertainment content. Today it has over 12 million subscribers and a market capitalization of $7 billion. From 2005 to 2009, Netflix's revenue more than tripled, and its earnings have grown from virtually zero to $115.9 million. Even the recent financial crisis has not slowed its growth. From 2008 to 2009, the company's revenue went up 22%, and its EPS grew by a whopping 50%. The stock market clearly acknowledged the company's high growth potential by assigning the stock a rich P/E ratio above 50. On July 21, right before Netflix made its second-quarter earnings announcement, its stock price closed at $119.65 (see Figure 12.3).

After market close, Netflix announced its earnings of $0.80, which handily beat the consensus forecast of $0.68. But Netflix missed the revenue forecast. It reported total revenue of $519.8 million, a 27% increase from last year, yet fell short of analysts' expectation of $524.1 million. The stock was hammered, dropping more than 9% after hours.

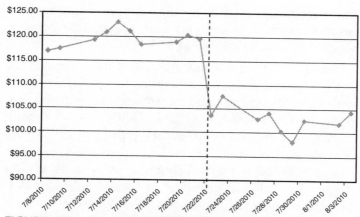

FIGURE 12.3 *Netflix (NASDAQ: NFLX) stock price in the 20 trading days surrounding the earnings announcement*

Here we have a growth company that easily beat earnings expectations but missed the consensus revenue target of $524.1 million by $4.3 million—a mere 0.8% miss. However, this slight miss essentially caused the stock price to tank as if it had been hit by a torpedo. The stock closed the next day at $103.56, a 13.4% decline. How could such a small 0.8% miss in expected revenues cause a 13.4% decline in market capitalization? Because growth companies face the added uncertainty of being a trailblazer in their industry or the market, they are particularly susceptible to small misses in revenues and earnings. These companies give the market insight into the future of such revenues and earnings streams.

Regardless, this example suggests that money can be made in putting on short positions in growth companies near their earnings announcement periods in the hopes that they miss—even by a hair—consensus earnings or revenue targets. At the very least, a straddle position would be quite profitable as well.

On July 22, at market close, Netflix's August 120 put was priced at $8.50 (see Figure 12.4). The next day, with earnings and revenue information impounded into prices, the put closed at $17.33. That's a 103.9% gain. If you were uncomfortable with putting a directional bearish put position in NFLX, a straddle position would have been pretty profitable as well. A similar August 120 call was priced at $8.10 and later closed at $1.12. So a straddle position would cost a total of $16.60. The next day, the value of this combined position was $18.45. That's a profit of 11.1%—a decent return without exposing yourself to directional risk.

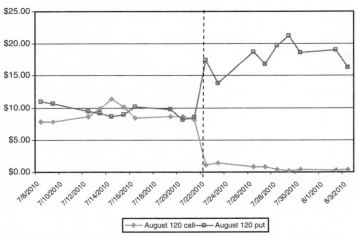

FIGURE 12.4   *NFLX August 120 call and August 120 put prices in the 20 trading days surrounding the earnings announcement*

Chapter 13

Revenue and Expense Surprises

This chapter discusses revenue and expense surprises. In recent years, it has become increasingly common for analysts to issue revenue forecasts along with their earnings forecasts. This has placed additional pressure on managers to meet not only earnings expectations, but also revenue expectations. Accounting earnings are nothing more than revenues minus expenses. So when a company announces earnings, if an earnings surprise occurs, by definition there must be either a revenue surprise or an expense surprise (or both). The subtler point is that a company can meet earnings expectations (that is, have an earnings surprise of zero) and yet still have revenue/expense surprises. Indeed, this has been the topic of recent conversations in the midst of the economic slowdown. Some companies are meeting earnings expectations—even though they are missing revenue expectations—because they are drastically cutting expenses proportionately. How important are these revenue and expense surprises?

Several recent studies have examined the interactions between earnings surprises and revenue and expense surprises. Ertimur, Livnat, and Martikainen (2003) found that the market reacted more strongly to revenue surprises than to expense surprises. Also, the market reacted more strongly when both earnings surprises and revenue surprises were in the same direction. (That is, a positive earnings surprise and positive revenue surprise occurred at the same time, or a negative earnings surprise and a negative revenue surprise occurred at the same time.) When the two had conflicting signs (a positive earnings surprise coupled with a negative revenue surprise, or vice versa), the market reaction was, on average, negative. In particular, when an earnings surprise was negative but the revenue surprise was positive (so expenses were larger than forecast), on average, the impact of the earnings surprise dominated the revenue surprise. On the other hand, when the earnings surprise was positive but the revenue surprise was negative, the market reaction depended on whether the company was a growth or value company. Specifically, for growth companies, a positive-earnings-but-negative-revenue surprise generally was met with a negative market reaction. In an environment where the market fixates on topline (revenue) growth—much like today's environment—revenue surprises can potentially dominate earnings surprises. Last, for value companies, these positive-earnings-but-negative-revenue surprises generally were met with positive market reactions. In another study, Jegadeesh and Livnat (2006) found that earnings announcement returns are related to *past* revenue surprises, as well as current revenue surprises. Thus, these findings provide a wealth of information about the types of surprises that matter. The market cares about the direction of revenue surprises, whether they are in the same direction as earnings surprises, and whether the surprise comes from a growth or value company.

Examples of revenue and expense surprises are plentiful. In fact, we already discussed a few of them. For instance, the Netflix example from the preceding chapter (Example 12.2) was precisely the case of a company that beat earnings expectations but missed its revenue target. Consistent with the findings just discussed, because Netflix is a growth company, this type of surprise was met with a severe negative market reaction.

Similar cases abound. For instance, on July 16, 2010 before the market opened, Bank of America (NYSE: BAC) announced its earnings for the second quarter of 2010. In the earnings announcement, BAC reported actual EPS of $0.27, which easily beat the consensus forecast of $0.22. This translated into a positive earnings surprise of $0.05, or 23%. However, Bank of America reported revenues for the quarter of $29.2 billion, which missed the $29.6 billion expected revenues by $0.4 billion, or −1.4%. These figures collectively suggest larger-than-anticipated expense reductions (since the bank's revenue missed the forecast but earnings beat the forecast). What was the market reaction to BAC's positive-earnings-but-negative-revenue surprise? BAC was trading more than 6% down as the market opened, and it closed the day down by more than 10%. Similarly (and on the same day), Citigroup (NYSE: C) also announced a positive earnings surprise, but its revenue fell short of the consensus forecast. The shares of

Citigroup went down more than 6% during the day. Option trading strategies here play out as we are getting used to seeing them play out. Let's close this chapter with one last example.

Example 13.1: Positive Earnings and Positive Revenue Surprise (NYSE: UPS)

United Parcel Service (NYSE: UPS) delivers packages each business day for 1.8 million shipping customers to 6.1 million consignees in over 200 countries and territories. On July 21, 2010, a day before its earnings announcement for the second quarter of 2010, UPS's stock price closed at $60.01 (see Figure 13.1).

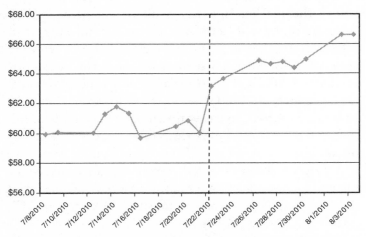

FIGURE 13.1   *United Parcel Service (NYSE: UPS) stock price in the 20 trading days surrounding the earnings announcement*

On July 22, UPS reported results that blew past both earnings and revenue expectations. Specifically, UPS reported a hefty actual $0.84 per share, which almost doubled the $0.44 per share from the same quarter last year and easily beat the consensus earnings expectation of $0.77 per share. On the revenue front, UPS reported total revenue of $12.2 billion, a 13% revenue increase over the same quarter last year, handily surpassing revenue expectations of $11.96 billion. That's a positive earnings *and* a positive revenue surprise.

The market rewarded UPS with a 5.2% increase in stock price, closing the day on July 22 at $63.15. Opening a straddle position the day before would have been profitable.

A long straddle position would entail purchasing an August 60 put for $2.17 and an August 60 call for $1.84, both on the day before the earnings announcement (see Figure 13.2). This would be a net investment of $4.01. On the day of the earnings announcement, the call increased in value to $3.85. The put, however, decreased in value to $0.84. This means that the value of our straddle after the earnings announcement is $4.69. That is a total gain of $0.68, a 16.9% gain.

As we discuss in Chapter 11, "Short Straddle and Strangle Strategies," opening the trade earlier typically is more expensive, with the straddle having a cost reaching as high as $4.84 in the 2 weeks prior to the earnings announcement. The only day that was cheaper for us to open the trade would have been the day before, July 21, when the straddle would have cost $4.01 (with the call priced at $1.84 and the put priced at $2.17). Choosing this perfect entry date is obviously difficult. On the other hand, allowing for an extension of the trade past its original exit date would have been quite profitable. Specifically, because the underlying equity price continued to plow upward in the coming days after the earnings announcement, the price of our straddle continued to rise as well. Specifically, although the August 60 put continued to lose value—fighting both the upward movement in the underlying equity as well as the power of time decay— the August 60 call steadily moved higher, overpowering any time decay effects. If we had closed the trade 5 days later, on July 28, the value of the straddle would have been $5.41 (calls worth $5.00 and puts worth $0.41). If we had closed the trade 10 days later, on August 3, the value of the straddle would have been $6.75 (calls worth $6.60 and puts worth $0.15). The usual caveats apply with attempts to time the market and the particular evils of time decay in front-month contracts.

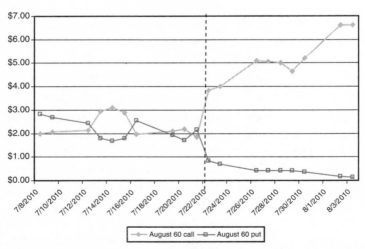

FIGURE 13.2   *UPS August 60 call and August 60 put prices in the 20 trading days surrounding the earnings announcement*

Chapter 14

Earnings Surprise Persistence

As we discussed with the examples of Apple and Ford Motor Company in Chapter 4, "Earnings Surprises: Empirical Evidence," analysts sometimes seem to consistently underestimate (or overestimate) earnings for some companies. Are these two examples merely a coincidence? Or do they reflect a broader empirical pattern? How common are companies that *persistently* report earnings surprises? Can Apple continue to blow away expectations quarter after quarter? Put differently, how much can we learn about future earnings surprises by examining past earnings surprises?

We set out to answer this question by examining the data. Specifically, we calculated the earnings surprises for all Russell 1000 companies during the period between July 1984 and December 2009. We then tabulated the chronological order, quarter by quarter, of earnings surprises for each company.

Our first analysis simply calculated the probability of a company's reporting a positive earnings surprise if it reported a positive earnings surprise in the previous quarter. Similarly, we calculated the probability of a negative earnings surprise if the company reported a negative earnings surprise in the past quarter. (We call these *same-sign* earnings surprises because positive surprises lead to positive surprises, and negative surprises lead to negative surprises.) Figure 14.1 shows that if a company reported a negative surprise in the previous quarter, the probability of reporting another negative surprise in the current quarter is 48.3%. If a company reported a positive surprise in the previous quarter, the probability of reporting another positive surprise in the current quarter is 76.1%. This initial evidence suggests that positive earnings surprises are relatively more persistent than negative earnings surprises. Put differently, we're much more likely to see a positive earnings surprise repeated than we are to see a negative earnings surprise repeated.

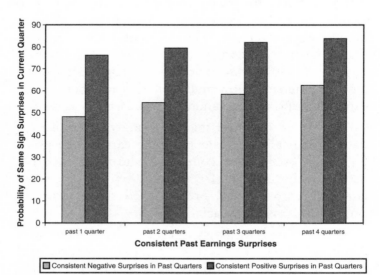

FIGURE 14.1   *Persistent earnings surprises over five consecutive quarters: the probability of the current quarter's earnings surprise direction given past quarters' earnings surprise direction*

In our second layer of analysis, we gathered all the companies that had *two* previous quarters of consecutive positive or negative earnings surprises. We then assessed whether the two previous same-sign surprises help predict the current quarter's surprise. The results are similar in spirit to the preceding test, where we required only one previous quarter's performance. In this case, again positive earnings surprises are more persistent than negative earnings surprises. However, now we have additional information when comparing the one-quarter requirement to the two-quarter requirement. Specifically, the probability of a same-sign surprise *increases* when we require two previous quarters versus one previous quarter. The probability of a positive surprise is now 79.6% for companies that had two consecutive previous quarters of positive surprises. Similarly, the probability of a negative surprise is now 54.8% when two consecutive negative surprises occurred.

We performed two additional layers of analysis, essentially adding to the prior requirements. The bars on the far right show the probability of a positive earnings surprise for firms that reported *four* consecutive past positive earnings surprises. The figure shows the same thing for negative surprises. We find that the probability of a positive earnings surprise is 83.9% if the company reported four prior quarters of positive earnings surprises. Similarly, the probability is 62.6% for negative surprises.

Scanning Figure 14.1 from left to right, we find that the probability of a particular signed earnings surprise gradually increases as the number of prior quarters of similar-signed surprises increases. For instance, the probability of a positive earnings surprise increases from 76.1% to 80.0% to 82.0% to 83.9%. This suggests that the more positive earnings surprises a company reports in the prior quarters, the more likely it is to report positive earnings in the current quarter. Similarly, the probability of a negative earnings surprise increases from 48.3% to 54.8% to 58.5% to 62.6%. Overall, the evidence suggests that earnings surprises are *persistent*.

Practically speaking from an options-trading point of view, this means that companies that have positively surprised the market with better-than-expected earnings in the past are *more likely* to positively surprise us again in the future. Similarly, companies that have consistently disappointed us in the past are more likely to disappoint us in the future. Needless to say, past performance does not guarantee future performance, but at least for earnings surprises, it does seem to increase the chances. These findings suggest that, for traders who want to make directional plays around earnings announcements (notwithstanding the caveats discussed in Chapter 6, "Market Reactions to Earnings Surprises (Are Full of Surprises)," the odds of winning can be significantly improved with companies that have something of a track record of past surprises. Let's look at an example.

Example 14.1: Persistent Positive Earnings Surprises (NYSE: F)

Ford Motor Company (NYSE: F) is one of the biggest manufacturers of cars and trucks in the world. Through the recent financial crisis, Ford was the sole survivor of the three auto giants. Since then, it has progressed toward restructuring its product lines and organization. Its recent string of results in 2009 and 2010 have surprised many skeptics of the company, consistently reporting earnings that beat analysts' consensus forecasts. For instance, the last three quarters have been good news. In September 2009, Ford beat EPS expectations of –$0.12 with an actual EPS of $0.38. Later, in December 2009, it again beat EPS expectations of $0.26 with an actual EPS of $0.43. Then, in March 2010, it surprised the market one more time with an actual EPS of $0.46 when expectations were only $0.31. These are three positive surprises in a row. So what might we expect for the most recent quarter, with earnings announced in July 2010? If we believe that earnings surprises tend to be persistent, we would expect another positive surprise.

On July 22, 2010, the day before Ford's second-quarter earnings announcement, its stock price closed at $12.09 (see Figure 14.2). The consensus estimate for EPS was $0.41 per share.

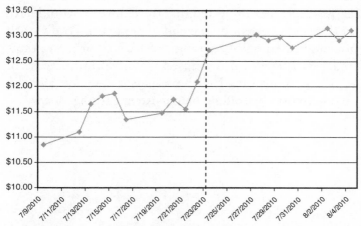

FIGURE 14.2   *Ford Motor Company (NYSE: F) stock price in the 20 trading days surrounding the earnings announcement*

It's important to note that the findings about earnings surprise persistence we've discussed suggest that we would again expect a positive surprise here. This is therefore a context in which we would open a directional position, not a typical straddle position in which we typically are indifferent about the direction of the stock price movement. The August 12 call closed at $0.65. Let's assume that we predict a positive earnings surprise and therefore purchase 30 call contracts, costing us $1,950.

On July 23, 2010, bolstered by strong sales of its new Fusion and redesigned Taurus models, Ford announced its earnings of $0.68 per share, with a consensus forecast of $0.40 per share (see Figure 14.3), again batting it out of the park. For Ford, earnings surprises seem to be persistently positive. This latest earnings performance was a 13% increase in profits and represented the best results in 6 years. Moreover, the automaker's share of the U.S. market improved from 16.9% to 17.2% over the last quarter. Management projected that the company would have more cash than debt by the end of next year. Ford's stock price increased 5.2%, closing at $12.72. For the options trade, its August call increased to $0.98, an increase of $0.33 per contract. This represents a gain of $990, a 50.8% return, by trading on persistent earnings surprises.

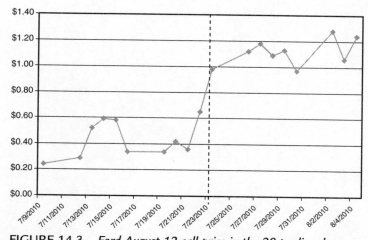

FIGURE 14.3 *Ford August 12 call price in the 20 trading days surrounding the earnings announcement*

Chapter 15

Other Theories and Evidence

A number of other theories and findings can guide your options trading. Some of these theories will help you directly with particular trading ideas, and others will simply help you better understand the environment in which you're placing your trades. *All* the studies' findings are backed by empirical evidence from hundreds of thousands of data points. This chapter summarizes some of these findings.

Richness of the Information Set

The market's reaction to an earnings surprise depends on how much the market is anticipating a company's earnings news. The richer and more complete a company's information environment, the smaller the market's reaction to the company's earnings surprise. Conversely, the more incomplete, obscure, and opaque the information surrounding a company is, the larger the market's reaction will be. Many studies have found that a firm's size—measured by its market capitalization, total assets, or total revenues—is a good indicator of the richness of the information set within which the company operates. Similarly, the greater the number of sell-side analysts who follow the company and the higher the level of institutional ownership, the better the information set. The reason is twofold. First, the presence of analysts and institutional investors means that more research reports (and earnings forecasts) are published about a company and are in the public domain. Second, the very presence of these analysts and institutions suggests that they have more power to demand information and transparency from the companies, thus compelling companies to provide more voluntary disclosures.

Compare this with small-cap companies that have few or no analysts following them. Such companies typically operate in an information environment that is fairly small. Thus, the earnings announcements that these types of companies make tend to attract a great deal of attention, because they are one of the only times and places where investors get their hands on information about the company. As a result, the market tends to react much more strongly to earnings surprises of these smaller, more obscure companies, simply because the market doesn't have much other information to react to.

The three measures are positively correlated because analysts and institutional investors tend to pay more attention to large-cap stocks than small-cap stocks. For example, Bank of America (NYSE: BAC) is one of the largest domestic banks, with over $150 billion market capitalization at the time of writing. It is followed by more than 25 analysts and is 64% owned by institutional investors. However, the correlation among the three measures is far from perfect. For instance, General Electric (NYSE: GE) has over $160 billion market capitalization, which is $10 billion larger than Bank of America, but it is followed by only 14 analysts, many fewer than the number of analysts following BAC. Moreover, its institutional ownership is just 30%, lower than many stocks with only 10% of its market capitalization. This example suggests that investors should examine all three measures when evaluating a stock's visibility. In our opinion, analyst following and institutional ownership are perhaps more important determinants of the market's reactions to earnings surprises than firm size, because analysts and professional investors are actively creating and acting on new information.

Practically speaking, this discussion suggests that volatility-based option trades such as straddles will work best with smaller companies, where the underlying stock price reaction tends to be larger and therefore makes straddle strategies more profitable. Of course, it's not all good news. Unfortunately, smaller, less-followed companies are simply less likely to have listed options. (We talk about this in Chapter 7, "General Characteristics of Optioned Companies and Options Behavior Around Earnings Announcements.") And even when such companies do have listed options, the trading volume for the contracts tends to be fairly low, which means that the bid-ask spreads are quite large. These large spreads significantly reduce the possibility of making profitable trades, because the movements of the option price must fight against the bid-ask spread that you must incur to open and close the trade. Nonetheless, we need not talk in black and white. The fact is that *relatively* smaller companies that have listed options and decent trading volume are more likely to be profitable with earnings-announcement-related straddle positions than *relatively* larger companies.

Predictable Biases in Analysts' Earnings Forecasts

Although analysts are very good at what they do and have incredible resources to do their job, in the end they are human and can make mistakes. Many studies refer to these mistakes as *biases*. Let's discuss.

The first type of bias found in analysts' earnings forecasts is an optimism-turns-to-pessimism bias. A long list of studies document analysts' tendency to issue optimistic forecasts (Fried and Givoly, 1982; O'Brien, 1988; Francis and Philbrick, 1993). A recent study published by McKinsey Consulting in 2010 reconfirms the age-old finding. Specifically, analysts tend to issue overly optimistic forecasts early in the year. However, as the fiscal year-end approaches, analysts tend to revise their earnings downward. By the time earnings are announced, analysts typically have revised their earnings so much lower that, on average, the earnings surprises are positive (Brown, 2001). This is part of the walk-down expectations guidance phenomenon we discuss in Chapter 3, "Earnings Surprises: Definition and Measurement." Analysts start their initial targets high, but then managers proceed to slowly, slyly walk those estimates down to more achievable levels by the end of the year. Perhaps this persistent pattern of downward earnings revisions partially explains why market reactions to positive earnings surprises are not always positive.

The second type of bias found in analysts' earnings forecasts is an underreaction bias. Specifically, analysts have been found to not fully impound—that is, they've been found to underreact to—certain types of information into their forecasts. For instance, a study by Mendenhall (1991) found that, when analysts forecast future earnings, they tended to underreact to the information contained in quarterly earnings announcements. That is, they seemed to only partially process the good or bad news found in the current earnings announcement. Similarly, Abarbanell (1991) found that analysts tended to underreact to the information that is embedded in past price changes. Gleason and Lee (2003) found that analysts underreacted to past earnings forecast revisions. Jegadeesh and Livnat (2006) found that analysts underreacted to revenue surprises. Basu, Markov, and Shivakumar (2010) found that analysts underreacted to the implication of inflation for future earnings. Perhaps analysts both underreact and overreact to information, depending on the nature of the information. Consistent with this view, Easterwood and Nutt (1999) found that analysts overreacted to good news but underreacted to bad news. Meanwhile, DeBondt and Thaler (1990) found that analysts' forecasts were too extreme, suggesting that they overreact to earnings news.

Is there a way to profit from these predictable biases in analysts' forecasts? A study conducted by Hughes, Liu, and Su (2008) found that the mistakes and biases in analysts' forecasts could actually be predicted using statistical forecasting methods. However, when simulated trading strategies were implemented to exploit these mistakes and biases in analysts' forecasts, the authors found that the strategies were not profitable. They concluded that the predictable component of earnings surprises was already reflected in the stock prices. To the extent that these findings for stock-trading strategies translate into similar options-trading strategies, these studies reinforce our view that directional bets on earnings surprises are fairly risky. Investors should focus more on straddle/strangle strategies that do not require making directional predictions.

Divergence of Opinions

As discussed in Chapter 3, we use analysts' consensus forecasts to measure earnings expectations. This is typically in the form of the average (mean) or median earnings forecast among all the analysts who issue such a forecast. However, this mean/median forecast can significantly mask the large differences in predictions that come from each analyst. Estimates can swing wildly. Sometimes the range of estimates—or divergence of opinions—can be enormous. For example, 40 analysts issued a forecast for Apple's (NASDAQ: AAPL) 2010 third-quarter earnings ending June 30, 2010. The average estimate is $3.07 per share, but the lowest estimate is only $2.65 and the highest estimate is $3.47. The difference between the highest and lowest estimate is a whopping $0.82, which is 27% of the average forecast. Not all companies have such a large dispersion in forecasts. For instance, 11 analysts issued a forecast for Coca-Cola's (NYSE: KO) 2010 third-quarter earnings, ending June 30, 2010. The average estimate is $1.03, the lowest estimate is $1.00, and the highest estimate is $1.05. The difference between the highest and lowest estimate is merely $0.05, which is about 5% of the average estimate. This is obviously a much tighter range.

Why do analysts have a much larger divergence of opinions for the earnings of Apple than for the earnings of Coca-Cola? Typical of a high-tech computer company, Apple's business is very dynamic and subject to the influence of many factors, including fierce competition from other smart phone and laptop manufacturers, the introduction of new products, and the constant testing of changing consumer tastes and preferences. These factors make it relatively more difficult to predict Apple's performance, and this fact is reflected in the wide range of earnings forecasts. On the other hand, Coca-Cola is a soft drink company with over 100 years of history. Consumer tastes for soft drinks are much more stable, as is customer loyalty. The level of soft drink consumption over time is also much less erratic and easier to predict, without any significant short-term spikes. These factors suggest that Coca-Cola's business is much more predictable.

Divergence of opinions thus reflects an investment's uncertainty. How does this uncertainty affect stock valuation? Miller (1977) developed a theory that stocks with more uncertainty tend to be overvalued because of constraints on short sales. The idea is that if uncertainty about a stock is high, the investor with the most optimistic view of the company will be the marginal buyer of its stock and hence set the stock price. Investors who are bearish about a company cannot counter the force of the optimistic investors, because they cannot effectively short the company's stock. As a result, stocks with high uncertainty are likely to be overvalued. Diether,

Malloy, and Scherbina (2002) used analysts' forecast dispersion to measure divergence of opinions. They found that, consistent with Miller's prediction, stocks with high divergence of opinions (a high level of dispersion in forecasts) tend to earn lower returns.

What is the impact of divergence of opinions on earnings announcement returns? Earnings announcements—in particular, earnings surprises—help resolve the uncertainty about a company and its performance. If stocks with high divergence of opinions are in general overvalued, earnings announcements are likely to pull them back to earth a little. This is exactly the finding of a recent study by Berkman, Dimitrov, Jain, Koch, and Tice (2009). These researchers found that earnings announcement returns generally are lower for stocks with high divergence of opinions. Moreover, consistent with Miller's prediction, earnings announcement returns are significantly lower for stocks that have a high divergence of opinions and tight short-sale constraints. Practically speaking, this suggests a directional, bearish strategy using options. You should certainly perform your due diligence with other aspects of the trade. But the evidence here suggests that long put positions in companies with a high level of forecast dispersion (and above-average difficulty in shorting the stock) may be profitable during earnings announcement periods.

Post-Earnings-Announcement Drift (PEAD)

The last topic of this chapter is a phenomenon called *post-earnings-announcement drift* (PEAD). The earliest study that documented this drift is the now-famous Ball and Brown (1968) study. Numerous later studies using different statistical methodologies and different samples have confirmed the existence of the drift. The drift has also been found in several other countries.[1] And as we discuss in detail next, this PEAD phenomenon can be quite large in terms of stock returns. The reason we have not covered this topic until now is because it is a *long-term* strategy, and the whole basis of our book has been *short-term* strategies. Nonetheless, we think it is important enough that it is worth discussing.

Thus far, we have focused on the market's reactions to an earnings surprise before or around an earnings announcement. However, the market's reaction to an earnings surprise does not end with the earnings announcement. In fact, the PEAD studies show that the market has a strong tendency to extend its reaction to an earnings surprise long after the current announcement. Specifically, stocks with strong positive earnings surprises tend to earn significantly higher returns *several quarters after* the current quarterly announcement. Similarly, stocks with large negative earnings surprises tend to earn much lower returns for the next several quarters. Essentially, the PEAD phenomenon shows that a firm with a very good earnings surprise not only gets a bump in its price on the day the announcement is made but also continues to see an upward *drift* in its price in the days, weeks, and months after the announcement is made. It's almost as if the market has trouble figuring out the full impact of the good news and needs a bit of time—a lot of time, apparently—to sufficiently figure things out. The same is true for bad news: A firm with a very bad earnings surprise continues to see a downward drift in its price in the months after earnings announcement day. This pattern is the PEAD. This drift can be quite large. Depending on the sample and methodology, the annual returns of a *zero-cost* hedge portfolio that is long the stocks with the largest positive earnings surprises and short the stocks with the largest negative earnings surprises can be more than 10%.

Researchers have proposed many explanations for the PEAD. Some researchers believe that the drift reflects some kind of unaccounted-for risk. For example, a study by Mendenhall (2004) found that the drift is correlated with arbitrage risk, the risk faced by arbitrageurs in the market who trade the drift. A study by Chordia, Goyal, Sadka, Sadka, and Shivakumar (2009) found that the drift occurs mainly in highly illiquid stocks, suggesting that liquidity risk is the reason behind the drift. Similar to the liquidity risk argument, Ng, Rusticus, and Verdi (2008) found that PEAD is concentrated around stocks with high transaction costs, which can significantly reduce the gains from a drift strategy. Both of these attributes are common among smaller-cap stocks. Other researchers think that the post-earnings announcement drift is caused by the market participants' inefficiency in processing earnings information. For example, Bernard and Thomas (1989) and Abarbanell and Bernard (1992) suggest that investors and analysts systematically underreact to information in the current earnings surprises for future earnings surprises. Companies with positive earnings surprises now tend to have positive earnings surprises in the future; the same is true of negative surprises. This is exactly the point we made in the preceding chapter regarding the persistence of earnings surprises. However, if investors and analysts don't see or realize this persistence, they may be repeatedly surprised in the same way in future quarters.

One *crucial* fact is that a disproportionate fraction of the drift is concentrated around future earnings announcements. This finding also confirms the idea that the market may be repeatedly surprised, quarter after quarter, by a company's quarterly earnings announcements. It's also possible that investors' limited attention in assessing information contributes to the PEAD. Consistent with this, Hirshleifer, Lim, and Teoh (2009) found that the PEAD is larger for stocks that announce earnings on days when many other stocks also announce earnings. This suggests that investors are overwhelmed with information overload and thus may not have the proper resources to fully assess and impound earnings-related information into stock prices. Similarly, Dellavigna and Pollet (2009) found that the drift is larger for earnings announcements that take place on Fridays because investors (focused on the coming weekend) seem to pay less attention to Friday announcements. Last, a study by Corrado and Truong (2009) found that PEAD tends to be less pronounced for firms that have abnormally high options trading volume in the preannouncement/announcement period. This suggests that the more action there is on the front end of the announcement, the less of a delayed reaction there is on the back end.

How might we capitalize on this PEAD with options trading strategies? As we've mentioned, this PEAD is largely a long-term phenomenon, but it does seem to be concentrated around the short time frames *after* earnings announcements. Even without considering the difference in time frames, you'll note that this is quite different from the options strategies we've been discussing thus far. Our trades have been opened *before* the earnings announcement, whereas the PEAD is a *post*-earnings phenomenon. The other big difference is that for an options-based PEAD strategy, we essentially already know the direction of the earnings surprise and market reaction.

Thus, the trading strategy is to wait for an earnings announcement to take place. Given the evidence just discussed, to maximize the probability of a profitable trade, you should select a relatively smaller company that announces earnings on the same day as many other companies or on a neglected Friday and that perhaps has relatively high trading volume in the preannouncement period. After it is announced, if the earnings surprise is a particularly large one (remember that small surprises do not exhibit PEAD), we could simply open a long, directional put or call in the direction of the market reaction. By definition, we pay more for the option after the announcement than we would before the announcement. That's because we are *reacting* to the sharp stock price movement, which necessarily makes the option more expensive than the day before the news was released. We then hold onto the position for a few days to capture the drift in the PEAD, which has been documented to be concentrated around the earnings announcement date. A further advantage of this PEAD strategy is that it exploits any volatility collapse that occurs in the postannouncement period.[2]

This trading strategy, which essentially rides the momentum or trend of the recent earnings announcement, is consistent with the findings of a recent study by Pan and Poteshman (2006). Examining proprietary trading data, they found that proprietary traders who work for investment houses open options positions that take advantage of the momentum or drift in returns. Individual investors tend to do the opposite, putting on options positions that trade against momentum. For instance, the authors found that individual investors will buy put options after a very large increase in price, expecting a price reversal. You, on the other hand, armed with knowledge of PEAD, will be taking advantage and riding the momentum, not fighting it.

Endnotes

1. *PEAD is also found in other countries, such as Finland, the UK, and Spain (Booth, Kallunki, and Martikainen, 1996; Liu, Strong, and Xu, 2003; and Forner, Sanabria, and Marhuenda, 2009).*

2. *However, be cautious of bid-ask spreads, because open interest and trading volume have been documented to decrease in this period as well (Donders et al., 2000).*

References

Abarbanell, J. 1991. "Do analysts' earnings forecasts incorporate information in prior stock price changes?" *Journal Accounting Research* (14): 147-166.

————and V. Bernard. 1992. "Tests of analysts' overreaction/underreaction to earnings information as an explanation for anomalous stock price behavior." *Journal of Finance* (47): 1181-1207.

Admati, A. and P. Pfleiderer. 1988. "A theory of intraday patterns: Volume and price variability." *Review of Financial Studies* 1(1): 3-40.

Amin, K. and C. Lee. 1997. "Option trading, price discovery, and earnings news dissemination." *Contemporary Accounting Research* (14): 153-192.

Ball, R. and P. Brown. 1968. "An empirical evaluation of accounting income numbers." *Journal of Accounting Research* (2): 159-178.

Basu, S., S. Markov, and L. Shivakumar. 2010. "Inflation, earnings forecasts, and post-earnings announcement drift." *Review of Accounting Studies* (15): 403-440.

Beaver, W. 1968. "The information content of annual earnings announcements." *Journal of Accounting Research* (6): 67-92.

Berkman, H., V. Dimitrov, P. Jain, P. Koch, and S. Tice. 2009. "Sell on the news: Differences of opinion, short-sales constraints, and returns around earnings announcements." *Journal of Financial Economics* (92): 376-399.

Bernard, V. and J. Thomas. 1989. "Post-earnings-announcement drift: Delayed price response or risk premium?" *Journal of Accounting Research* (27): 1-36.

Black, F. and M. Scholes. 1973. "The pricing of options and corporate liabilities." *Journal of Political Economy* (81): 637-654.

Bonner, Sarah E., Artur Hugon, and Beverly R. Walther. 2007. "Investor Reaction to Celebrity Analysts: The Case of Earnings Forecast Revisions." *Journal of Accounting Research* 45(3): 481-513.

Booth, G., J. Kallunki, and T. Martikainen. 1996. "Post-earnings-announcement drift and income smoothing: Finnish evidence." *Journal of Business, Finance & Accounting* (23): 1197-1211.

Bradshaw, M. and R. Sloan. 2002. "GAAP versus the street: An empirical assessment of two alternative definitions of earnings." *Journal of Accounting Research* (40): 41-66.

Brown, L. 2001. "A temporal analysis of earnings surprises: Profits versus losses." *Journal of Accounting Research* (39): 221-241.

———and K. Sivakumar. 2003. "Comparing the value relevance of two operating income measures." *Review of Accounting Studies* (8): 561-572.

Cao, C., Z. Chen, and J. Griffin. 2005. "Information content of option volume prior to takeovers." *Journal of Business* (78): 1073-1109.

Chakravarty, S., H. Gulen, and S. Mayhew. 2004. "Informed trading in stock and option markets." *Journal of Finance* 59(3): 1235-1257.

Chan, K., Y. Chung, and W. Fong. 2002. "The information role of stock and option volume." *The Review of Financial Studies* (15): 1049-1075.

Chen, T. and Z. Gu. 2004. "Analysts' treatment of non-recurring items in street earnings." *Journal of Accounting & Economics* (38): 129-170.

Chordia, T., A. Goyal, G. Sadka, R. Sadka, and L. Shivakumar. 2009. "Liquidity and the post-earnings-announcement drift." *Financial Analysts Journal* (65): 18-32.

Corrado, C. and C. Truong. 2009. "Options trading volume and stock price response to earnings announcements." Working paper.

DeBondt, W. and R. Thaler. 1990. "Do security analysts overreact?" *American Economic Review* (80): 52-57.

Dellavigna, S. and J. Pollet. 2009. "Investor inattention and Friday earnings announcements." *Journal of Finance* (64): 709-749.

Diether, K., C. Malloy, and A. Scherbina. 2002. "Differences of opinion and the cross section of stock returns." *Journal of Finance* (57): 2113-2141.

Donders, M., R. Kouwenberg, and T. Vorst. 2000. "Options and earnings announcements: An empirical study of volatility, trading volume, open interest and liquidity." *European Financial Management* 6(2): 149-171.

Doyle, J., R. Lundholm, and M. Soliman. 2003. "The predictive value of expenses excluded from Pro Forma earnings." *Review of Accounting Studies* (8): 145-174.

Easley, D., M. O'Hara, and P. Srinivas. 1998. "Option volume and stock prices: Evidence on where informed traders trade." *Journal of Finance* (53): 431-465.

Easterwood, J. and S. Nutt. 1999. "Inefficiency in analysts' earnings forecasts: Systematic misreaction or systematic optimism?" *Journal of Finance* (54): 1777-1797.

Ertimur, Y., J. Livnat, and M. Martikainen. 2003. "Differential market reactions to revenue and expense surprises." *Review of Accounting Studies* (8): 185-211.

Forner, C., S. Sanabria, and J. Marhuenda. 2009. "Post-earnings announcement drift: Spanish evidence." *Spanish Economic Review* (11): 207-241.

Francis, J. and D. Philbrick. 1993. "Analysts' decisions as products of a multi-task environment." *Journal of Accounting Research* (31): 216-230.

Fried, D. and D. Givoly. 1982. "Financial analysts' forecasts of earnings: A better surrogate for market expectations." *Journal of Accounting & Economics* (4): 85-107.

Gleason, C. and C. Lee. 2003. "Analyst forecast revisions and market price discovery." *The Accounting Review* (78): 193-225.

Hirshleifer, D., S. Lim, and S. Teoh. 2009. "Driven to distraction: Extraneous events and underreaction to earnings news." *Journal of Finance* (64): 2289-2325.

Ho, J. 1993. "Option trading and the relation between price and earnings: A cross-sectional analysis." *The Accounting Review* (68): 368-384.

Hughes, J., J. Liu, and W. Su. 2008. "On the relation between predictable market returns and predictable analyst forecast errors." *Review of Accounting Studies* (13): 266-291.

Jegadeesh, N. and J. Livnat. 2006. "Revenue surprises and stock returns." *Journal of Accounting & Economics* (41): 147-171.

Jennings, R. and L. Starks. 1986. "Earnings announcements, stock price adjustment, and the existence of option markets." *Journal of Finance* 41(1): 107-126.

Kim, S. and J. Lee. 2006. "Effect of option listing on price reactions to earnings announcements." Working paper, University of Alberta.

Kinney, W., D. Burgstahler, and R. Martin. 2002. "Earnings surprise 'materiality' as measured by stock returns." *Journal of Accounting Research* (40): 1297-1329.

Landsman, W. and E. Maydew. 2002. "Has the information content of quarterly earnings announcements declined in the past three decades?" *Journal of Accounting Research* (40): 797-808.

Liu, W., N. Strong, and X. Xu. 2003. "Post-earnings-announcement drift in the UK." *European Financial Management* (9): 89-116.

Mendenhall, R. 2004. "Arbitrage risk and post-earnings-announcement drift." *Journal of Business* (77): 875-894.

———. 1991. "Evidence on the possible underweighting of earnings-related information." *Journal of Accounting Research* (29): 170-179.

———and D. Fehrs. 1999. "Option listing and the stock-price response to earnings announcements." *Journal of Accounting & Economics* (27): 57-87.

Miller, E. 1977. "Risk, uncertainty, and divergence of opinion." *Journal of Finance* (32): 1151-1168.

Mixon, P. 2009. "Option markets and implied volatility: Past versus present." *Journal of Financial Economics* (94): 171-191.

Ng, J., T. Rusticus, and R. Verdi. 2008. "Implications of transaction costs for the post-earnings announcement drift." *Journal of Accounting Research* (46): 669-696.

O'Brien, P. 1988. "Analysts' forecasts as earnings expectations." *Journal of Accounting & Economics* (10): 53-83.

Pan, J. and A. Poteshman. 2006. "The information in option volume for future stock prices." *Review of Financial Studies* (19): 871-908.

Park, Chul W., and Earl K. Stice. 2000. "Analyst forecasting ability and the stock price reaction to forecast revisions." *Review of Accounting Studies* (5): 259-272.

Patell, J. and M. Wolfson. 1979. "Anticipated information releases reflected in call option prices." *Journal of Accounting & Economics* (1): 117-140.

Roll, R., E. Schwartz, and A. Subrahmanyam. 2009. "Options trading activity and firm valuation." *Journal of Financial Economics* (94): 345-360.

Shon, J. 2009. "Do Earnings Surprises Affect Voluntary Disclosure Behavior? A Study of High-Tech Firms in Periods of Declining Stock Price." *Accounting and Taxation* 1(1): 1-13.

———and R. Weiss. 2009. "Voluntary Disclosure Behavior During Exogenous Crisis Events." *Journal of Applied Business and Economics* 9(4): 9-16.

———and P. Zhou. 2009. "Are earnings surprises interpreted more optimistically on sunny days? Accounting information and the sunshine effect." *Journal of Accounting, Auditing, and Finance* 24:2: 211-232.

———and P. Zhou. 2010. "Can Mispricing of Asset Growth Explain the Accruals Anomaly?" *International Journal of Business and Finance Research* 4(1): 73-83.

———and P. Zhou. 2010. "Do Divergent Opinions Explain the Value Premium?" *Journal of Investing* 19(2), 53-62.

Skinner, D. and R. Sloan. 2002. "Earnings surprises, growth expectations, and stock returns, or don't let an earnings torpedo sink your portfolio." *Review of Accounting Studies* (7): 289-312.

INDEX

FT Press
FINANCIAL TIMES

In an increasingly competitive world, it is quality of thinking that gives an edge—an idea that opens new doors, a technique that solves a problem, or an insight that simply helps make sense of it all.

We work with leading authors in the various arenas of business and finance to bring cutting-edge thinking and best-learning practices to a global market.

It is our goal to create world-class print publications and electronic products that give readers knowledge and understanding that can then be applied, whether studying or at work.

To find out more about our business products, you can visit us at www.ftpress.com.